THE VIKINGS IN THE ISLE OF MAN

THE VIKINGS IN
THE ISLE OF MAN

David M Wilson

AARHUS UNIVERSITY PRESS |

THE VIKINGS IN THE ISLE OF MAN
© The author and Aarhus University Press 2008
Designed, typeset and printed by Narayana Press, Gylling

Cover by Jørgen Sparre; photos © the author
Printed in Denmark 2008
ISBN 978 7934 370 2 (Pb)
ISBN 978 7934 367 2 (Hb)

Aarhus University Press
Langelandsgade 177
DK-8200 Aarhus N
www.unipress.dk

White Cross Mills
Hightown, Lancaster, LA1 4XS
United Kingdom
www.gazellebookservices.co.uk

PO Box 511
Oakville, CT 06779
www.oxbowbooks.com

Published with the financial support of
Manx Heritage Foundation

Contents

To Else, James and Leslie;
learned and candid friends.

Preface

This book has its origin more than sixty years ago. In 1944 I first came to live in the Isle of Man and for a short time my parents and I lodged in a house opposite the lychgate of Kirk Michael church. At that time this gate housed the Michael crosses and it was on these that I first met the Vikings through their ornament and inscriptions. This was the beginning of my interest in Viking-Age archaeology. Having written widely on the period, I now wish to repay my debt to the Island for delivering me into my life's academic path. The Island, through its archaeological remains concentrated in a confined space, is one of the most important sources for the history of the Viking settlement in the West and its remains form a unique testimony to the spirit of Scandinavian expansion at this period.

More prosaically, this book had its origin in a monstrously long chapter for the new History of the Isle of Man which I completed in 2002. This volume has not yet appeared and will be delayed for some time. But, as my views and knowledge of the subject changed, I withdrew the chapter and expanded it into this book, with a longer text and a richer body of pictures.

A few words of explanation must introduce this essay. First, conventions in relation to parish-names vary – parishes and parish-churches are often referred to in the literature with the appellative 'Kirk'. This is by no means universal and in some cases is just pedantic. Nobody in the Island refers to 'Kirk Marown' or 'Kirk Malew'; they drop the first element. 'Kirk Michael' is however a normal usage, although many refer to it in speech simply as 'Michael'. I have tried to follow modern written usage in this book, as I have for the name 'Onchan', which is sometimes lovingly referred to by antiquarians as 'Conchan'. Santon and Santan are interchangeable. I am aware that I have not been totally consistent, but that can only serve to tease pedants. Second, for the benefit of English readers, I have normalised Norse forms of proper names only when they appear in inscriptions and other contemporary sources, e.g. Heðinn. Other names are written in their received modern English form, e.g. Sigurd and not Sigurðr.

I have tried to avoid obscure technical terminology, but one or two uses may cause confusion. The term 'British Isles' is used here in its strictly geographical sense; not in any sense politically. There may, in the context of this book, be misunderstanding about the adjective 'insular'. This is usefully employed by students of the Viking Age to refer to the British Isles – it is a happier term than 'Hiberno-Saxon'. I never use the term 'insular' to refer to the Isle of Man.

Finally, a word about sources. I am an archaeologist by training and profession and much of the material used in this book, particularly the foundation building-blocks discussed in some detail in chapters 2 and 3, are drawn from archaeology, for in most respects this period of Manx history should be seen as 'prehistoric'. In a book of this nature, however, it is necessary to use sources other than those provided by my own specialism – disciplines which span everything from formal history to philology and numismatics. It is nowadays impossible for one person to use all these with equal skill. I have, therefore, where possible, checked with generous colleagues who are specialists in other subject areas, but there are bound to be errors, mainly (I hope) of nuance; for such errors I throw myself on the reader's charity. Further, because this study sets the Isle of Man in its Scandinavian context, some of the references are to publications in Scandinavian languages; there is no way I could avoid this, but such references are kept to the minimum, and many articles and books quoted have summaries in English.

I am particularly grateful to the late Robert Thomson for reading the linguistic portion of chapter 1 in draft and making many suggestions and corrections which modified my very black-and-white views as regards language. Raymond Page and Gillian Fellows-Jensen have been enormously helpful on runes and place-names. David Doyle helped me on Manx legal matters and Stefan Brink provided me with copies of two articles in advance of publication. Anne Pedersen, Sonja Marzinzik and Sarah Semple have been most generous of their time and willingly answered queries. Alison Fox and Andrew Johnson of Manx National Heritage have generously put their local knowledge at my disposal and helped me with photographs which Manx National Heritage has generously provided without copyright fee. I owe a great debt of gratitude (as do so many Manx scholars) to Charles Guard and the Manx Heritage Foundation for a generous grant towards the publication of this volume and for providing me with some splendid photographs specially taken by John Hall and the distribution map produced by Vic Bates. My wife has as usual helped with drawings and read and criticised an early draft of the book with exemplary patience. Marjorie Caygill, James Graham-Campbell and Else Roesdahl have also read drafts of the book and criticised it to my great advantage. They have saved me from many errors and suggested ways in which it could be improved. I find it difficult to express my thanks in sufficient and appropriate form for this help and for similar assistance over many years; suffice it say that without their help the book would never have appeared.

David M Wilson
Castletown, August 2007.

Acknowledgments

I am grateful to the following for providing illustrations: The Manx Heritage Foundation, figs 1, 56 (photos John Hall), 4 (map by Vic Bates). Manx National Heritage, figs. 7, 10, 11, 12, 14, 18, 24, 25, 32, 35, 37 left, 43, 44, 45, 51, 54, 55. The National Museum of Wales (drawing by Tony Daly), fig. 15. The Trustees of the British Museum, 50, 53. St Patrick's Isle Trust, figs. 20 and 21. The author, figs. 2, 3, 5, 13, 22, 23, 30, 31, 33, 34, 36, 37 right, 38, 39, 40, 41, 42, 48, 52, 59. The author and the late Gerhard Bersu, figs. 6, 8, 9, 16. Professor Timothy Darvill, fig. 58. The late Peter Gelling, fig. 47. The late Basil and Eleanor Megaw, fig. 60. Eva Wilson, figs. 17, 19, 26, 27, 28, 29, 49. I have been unable to trace the owner of the copyright of fig. 57.

Introduction

Terminology and identity

The Isle of Man is today chiefly known as an offshore Island with a major financial services industry. Many have only the vaguest idea of its position, topography or even its history; and yet its present independent prosperity is based on events which took place more than a thousand years ago when it came under Norse control and was ultimately established as a polity with its own legislature and constitution, which in a much modified form survives to this day. To historians of early medieval Scandinavia its importance as a Viking 'colony' has been much discussed and its role in the greater Scandinavian world of the period has been rigorously examined for nearly two centuries. Because of the wealth of its archaeological remains, its remarkable series of sculptured memorial stones, its place-names, and even its present-day legislature, it is seen by them as a useful microcosm of a settlement in the west and is much referred to in literature on almost all aspects of the Viking Age.

In this short book it is my intention to examine and try to explain the story of the Isle of Man in the period from the end of the ninth century to the middle of the eleventh century, when settlers of Scandinavian origin forged a kingdom, sometimes independent and sometimes a client of a greater power, which had a Norse identity. The story has been dredged from disparate and often obscure sources to provide a narrative for a general audience, supplemented by a critical apparatus which will I trust be of use to specialists. At the same time I shall attempt to place the island in its historical and cultural context in relation to the people and culture of the rest of the northern world.

In writing of this period one quickly becomes conscious of the need to define terms, for usage has changed over the centuries. Terms glibly used are now questioned on a regular basis by semantically oriented scholars with their own baggage. This hurdle has to be overcome. One of the problems facing any serious writer dealing with the Viking Age concerns the usage of the term 'Viking' itself, which I have used – if sparingly – in much of this book. The word 'Viking' did not come into general use in the English language until the middle of the nineteenth century – at about the same time that it was introduced into serious academic literature in Scandinavia – and has since then changed its meaning and been much abused. It must, however, be accepted that the term is today used throughout the world as a descriptor of the peoples of Scandinavia in the period from the late eighth century until the mid-eleventh century. To the general public, however, it has apparently two meanings; both are respectable and hallowed in the English language by two centuries of usage. The first is in the sense of 'raider' or 'pirate', the second in the sense of the activities of the Scandinavians outside their own country in that period. It is the latter meaning that has given rise to the useful term 'the Viking Age'. Disregarding the ultimate philology of the word and the history of its use over the centuries, which has been much discussed,[1] it is now in such everyday use by both specialists and non-specialists – however improperly – to describe the Scandinavians of the Viking Age, that it almost impossible to avoid its use in this generic sense. Although it is often appropriate and necessary to use such terms as 'Scandinavian' or 'Norse', as I have done in this book, it is often simpler and less confusing to label something as 'Viking' rather than deal in scholastic circumlocution to placate purists, however justified they may be in their arguments.[2] I have tried therefore to use all three terms in a fashion appropriate to a general readership – the term 'Viking' is too valuable and generally used to jettison now. The only serious caveat is that the word 'Viking' is a western European construct which many Russians and even Swedes, with justification, sometimes find hard to use in relation to Scandinavian activity in eastern Europe.

Similarly there are problems with national labels. Until quite late in the nineteenth century, the Vikings were labelled by British scholars as 'Danes' – a portmanteau term which embraced all Scandinavian influences of the Viking Age in Britain. This was an anglocentric view of the period based on the fact that the most important Scandinavian interventions in England from the beginning of the Viking Age to its end seem to have been driven from Denmark. It soon became evident that major influences also derived from Norway and, to a lesser extent, from Sweden. Nowadays, having accepted the term 'Viking', it is necessary to stress that in using the names of the three major Scandinavian countries in writing of the Viking Age, we are not referring to their political or ethnic structure in that period. We use them as terms of convenience. Only Denmark, a relatively small country, has any claim to be labelled as a kingdom in the early Viking Age, although its geographical extent at certain times (in relation to its control over the southern provinces of Norway and Sweden particularly) is only dimly perceived. 'Norway' and 'Sweden' are labels used by everybody writing about this period, but it must be emphasised that these countries were not single entities, but geographical regions made up of a shifting kaleidoscope of different kingdoms and earldoms, variously controlled until brought together in the course of the eleventh and twelfth centuries. Further, it must be remembered that a vast area of the north of both Norway and Sweden was the home of the semi-nomadic Sami (once known as Lapps), who were important in economic terms to their southern neighbours, but

---

1 It first re-emerges in English in 1807. Fell 1986 and 1987.
2 E.g. Nelson 2003, 28.

INTRODUCTION

whose material culture was very different.[3] The modern national terms are used here for convenience and not in a nationalist sense. What goes for Scandinavia is also true for the other countries of Europe, for this was a period of kaleidoscopic political change. The Low Countries, Spain, France, England, Ireland, Scotland, Wales, for example were all at various times split into smaller entities, but it would be tedious to try and detail them at every turn; they are here used purely in a present-day geographical sense – as is the term 'British Isles', which remains a convenient geographical term, although it is sadly being eroded by nationalist sentiment.

Another problem concerns ethnic identity. In describing the Viking Age in the Isle of Man it is almost possible to ignore this problem. Almost, but not quite. Inscriptions on tenth-century stones decorated in Viking taste show, as will be demonstrated, some sort of social relationship between the two elements of the population: the Vikings and those who were already established when they arrived. The native inhabitants were Celtic-speaking, but on the basis of the surviving evidence – epigraphic and toponymic – and by parallel with later Manx history it is clear that the Scandinavian language was dominant, and that their language was that of government. But throughout the Viking and later Norse (c.1079-1266) period it is probable that there was an under-class who continued to speak the old language, which was refreshed and altered when Man came under the control of the Scottish crown in the late thirteenth century. It is easy to say, but difficult to prove, that the two ethnic elements lived in harmony, but with social mobility fuelled by intermarriage, the accepted language – the only touchstone we have – became Norse. For the purposes of this book we can only be aware that there was a substantial element in the population – probably the majority in the Viking Age – which was non-Scandinavian. Scratch a Manxman today and he will automatically describe his ethnicity as 'Celtic', implying a close cultural and linguistic bond with the Scots, Irish, Welsh, Cornish and Bretons. In so doing he is emphasising his separation from the English; he is, however, more ambivalent about his relationship with Scandinavia (proud perhaps of a rather rakish image of Norse descent). The Manx *are* separate and distinct, that is the source of their strengths and of their weaknesses. But it must be pointed out that there are probably now – and were for some time in the past – more English elements in the Manx cultural make-up than Celtic. What the situation was in the Viking Age can only be a matter for conjecture. It is not the purpose of this book to fish in these muddy waters, but readers must be aware of the problem and of the controversial nature of Manx national identity after more than a thousand years of government by a non-Celtic-speaking ruling class, a situation which is much on the Manx political agenda today.

---

3 The literature on this subject is immense and increasing, but for an overview see Zachrisson 1993.

Fig. 1. The northern plain of the Isle of Man seen from North Barrule.
Spanning the parishes of Jurby, Andreas, Bride and Lezayre.

CHAPTER 1

The background – topographical and historical

The Isle of Man lies in the middle of the Irish Sea (fig. 4), towards its north-east corner, and is visible from all the lands which surround it. The sea – until recently perhaps the most important element in its independence and economy – is conditioned by tides and currents which present dangers to the unwary sailor. In winter its rugged coastline is lashed by storms (mainly from the south-west), which, with the currents, have provided some sort of protection against outside predators. In summer the sea has a benign appearance, but one that is often misleading as storms arise without warning and fog cloaks the Island in a manner which still puts sailors at risk from rocky shores and underwater outcrops.

The Island is roughly lozenge-shaped, about 45km long and up to 16km broad; it has an area of 572km². Its axis is roughly north-east/south-west and its landscape is dominated by two upland massifs divided by a central valley, which crosses the Island

Fig. 2. The Manx uplands. These inhospitable areas were encroached on by the incoming Vikings.

from Douglas in the east to Peel in the west. Seen from the British mainland and Ireland, it appears as a single mountain rising steeply from the sea; indeed, much of its land-mass consists of uplands which, in a series of rounded moors and hills, rise in the northern massif to a height of 621m (in the south to 483m). It is mainly formed of Ordovician slates or mudstones, with an outcrop of Carboniferous limestone in the south and a small source of Devonian sandstone in the west (around the present-day town of Peel). Other rocks also occur, including small, but significant, intrusive granite and dolerite.[1] The coastline is largely rocky and backed by cliffs, which have a few indentations providing beaches or anchorages for ships. But the limestone landfall of the south is less precipitate and provides the basis of a rich and fertile agricultural plain formed largely of sedimentary glacial deposits. The north (fig. 1) of the Island also has good low-lying agricultural land, consisting of complicated moraine deposits backing alluvial sands washed out of the last ice-cap, which have formed miles of sandy beaches. The uplands (fig. 2), on which none of the original vegetation survives, were largely deforested by the time the Vikings arrived *c.* 900 and are now bare, providing hill pasture for sheep where they are not planted with modern conifers. At the south-west tip of the Island is a rocky islet, the Calf of Man (fig. 3), separated from the mainland by the strong currents of a rocky sound.

---

1 For geology see Chadwick et al. 2001; Chiverrell and Thomas 2006.

Fig. 3. The promontory fort of Burroo Ned. Beyond are the Sound and the Calf of Man.

The first traces of human activity in Man date back to the Mesolithic period, some 10,000 years ago, at which time it was still connected by a land bridge to Cumbria and southern Scotland. The Island has been continuously occupied since. By the time of the birth of Christ, the Island had settled down to an economy based on farming and fishing, touched occasionally by merchants from the neighbouring islands and possibly occasionally threatened by marauders from across the seas. In the early centuries of the first millennium a number of defended houses were built on headlands (usually above convenient harbourages), as at the undated but impressive site of Burroo Ned (fig. 3) or Close ny Chollagh, Arbory (fig. 44), where four circular houses were found within a rampart. Many of these fortifications were used – probably intermittently – through the Viking Age into the Middle Ages.[2] During the early centuries of the first millennium the inhabitants lived in round houses of various forms and sizes, similar to those generally found in the western parts of the British Isles, and there is evidence that these were the dwellings encountered by the Scandinavians when they first arrived in the Island. The indigenous people were self-sufficient, and sophisticated enough, for example, to have a specialised metalworking industry.

In practically all aspects of the material culture and economic activity of the Isle of Man there is apparently an unbroken continuity from the centuries before the birth of Christ through to the arrival of the Vikings towards the end of the ninth century

---

2 For a general discussion of these fortifications see Johnson 2002.

(there is no evidence of Roman settlement and precious few documented Roman finds from the Island). The coming of Christianity, presumably at some time in the fifth century, introduced new elements which may be traced in the archaeological record. These consist, first, of a small number of inscribed and minimally decorated stone monuments, some of which are of explicitly Christian character; and, second (and much more enigmatic and difficult of interpretation), a number of cemeteries which are sometimes related to Christian chapels (known as *keeils*). While some of these keeils may belong to the pre-Viking era, recent excavation would suggest that they are generally of a tenth-century or later date. This evidence is supported by the presence of a fair number of similar sites in the western areas of the British Isles which, as in the Isle of Man, consist of small single-cell chapels surrounded by burial-grounds. Most such chapels (sometimes known as 'field churches') in mainland Britain are now believed to have been erected, sometimes on the site of pre-existing cemeteries, in the tenth or eleventh century.[3] Some, however, as at Heysham on the west coast of Lancashire almost within sight of the Isle of Man,[4] are certainly earlier. There can, moreover, be little doubt on the basis of inscriptional evidence, that there was a religious settlement (usually designated as a 'monastery'[5]) at Maughold on the east coast of the Isle of Man before the Viking Age and that it was probably founded in the seventh century.[6] This is attested by a number of memorial crosses, on one of which is an inscription in a Latin book-hand of the eighth or ninth century, which in translation reads '[in the name of] Jesus Christ, Branhui brought water to this place'. This inscription alone would imply an established Christian community before the coming of the Vikings.

Early documentation and epigraphy

It might be expected that, as the Romans arrived in the British Isles towards the end of the first century, the literacy which accompanied them would produce records or at least mentions of the Island. But even here there is a problem in that the name for Man has for many years been confused with that of Anglesey (modern Welsh, *Mon*). It is now universally accepted that the occurrence of this name in the works of Caesar in the first century BC refers to Anglesey, as almost certainly does the term *Menavia* in the sixth-century Ravenna cosmography. Bede's record of the conquest of 'Man' by Edwin of Northumbria (616-32),[7] probably refers to the Isle of Man, as the text refers

---

3 For the re-dating of these churches see Blair 2005, 374ff.
4 Potter and Andrews 1994.
5 For a crisp discussion of such terminology in England see Blair 2005, 3-5, 18-22. It is possible, however, that Maughold was more closely locked into the Irish pattern, where monastic establishments were more common and clearly discernible; see Hughes 2005.
6 Wilson 2008.
7 *HE*, II, cap.ix.

to two separate islands (the larger of which lies to the south). Whether, however, the writer was reflecting an actual historical event may be questioned, although both English and Irish historians seem to accept it, and the latter assume that the power of the Ulaid kings of northern Ireland was thereby reduced.[8] The reference in Nennius's *Historia Brittonum, c.* 816, to '*Eubonia* which is *Manau*', could confuse the two islands, although the context (*in umbilico maris inter hiberniam et bryttanniam* – in the middle of the sea between Ireland and Britain) certainly favours Man.[9] Likewise, a sixth-century reference in the Annals of Ulster to *Eufania,* almost certainly refers to Man, in view of the geographical propinquity of Ulster and Man.[10] There are dim and sometimes legendary references to what must be the Island in various Irish annals and sagas before the coming of the Vikings;[11] while in the eighth-century Welsh saga, *Compert Mongáin,* there is the first reference to the sea-god Manannán mac Lir, who (as a giant) is an important figure in Manx folk-lore.[12] The first indisputable mention of the Isle of Man under that name (*maun*) is written in Norse runes on a tenth-century stone memorial cross from Kirk Michael (below, fig. 26 and p. 63).[13]

No written sources from the Island itself relate to this period, save for a small number of inscriptions carved on stone.[14] These, however difficult of interpretation, provide important evidence of a period, broadly dated from the fifth to the ninth century, which saw the introduction and establishment of Christianity, a religion which replaced the assumed polytheism of the late Iron Age. Three scripts are used. First, the Latin alphabet; second, ogham (an alphabet of twenty letters made up of groups of short lines set at different angles in relation to a median base-line), which is found in all the lands around the Irish Sea, although principally in the south of Ireland; and, third, the runic alphabet. This latter is a general Germanic script in which each individual character is made up of one or more straight lines (with a few curved ones), which in the Island first appears in its Anglo-Saxon form. A Norwegian version of the script was introduced by the Viking incomers in the tenth century, and is discussed in chapter 3.

---

8 Ó Cróinín 2005, 218.
9 Dumville 1985, 63.
10 *S.a.* 576 (corrected date, 577).
11 Byrne 1973, 109-10; Woolf forthcoming.
12 Charles-Edwards 2000, 202.
13 The late Robert Thomson kindly informed me (letter, 16 Nov 2002) that, '... it seems that the names of both islands were the same in origin but transmitted to us in the two forms of Insular Celtic, i.e. Goidelic and Brythonic. Brythonic is the more rapidly evolving of the two... The Latinised version was *Manav(i)a*; Brythonic retains this ending in its name for Man, viz *Manaw*, but drops it in the name for Anglesey, Mon. ... The runic *maun*... no doubt represents Mön, but Man seems to have come down from Old English Manu. Manx *Mannin* repesents [the accusative/dative]'.
14 The most convenient and useful re-examination of these inscriptions is in an unpublished Ph.D thesis – Trench-Jellicoe 1985.

All the pre-Viking-age inscriptions are of a memorial nature, bearing, for example, the name of a person and his paternity. Although useless as detailed historical sources, the temptation to identify some of the named people with historical persons has – to some scholars – proved almost irresistible.[15] In more sceptical times, the fact that we might not accept an historical identity for persons memorialised in the inscriptions does not mean that Manx texts are without significance, for they enable us to recognize the presence of Christian people related by their script or language to communities in the various regions around the Irish Sea. In some cases it is possible to date the inscriptions on the basis of epigraphy or associated ornament – within, it must be admitted, a broad range. Further, in a limited manner, the inscriptions illuminate life on the Island at this period (for example, the reference to water being brought to Maughold, quoted above).

These early memorial stones are generally found in cemeteries. Their Christian identity is confirmed in most cases by the presence of a cross or a specifically Christian inscription. Influences in their carving are drawn from all the countries around the Irish Sea. The few Welsh elements seem to be early and, while there are Irish parallels, they are masked by Scottish influence, most importantly from South-West Scotland. Some Manx stones influenced from this area drew on an English tradition, and, while Pictish elements in Man are indisputable, the route by which they arrived in the Island is obscure.

English influence in Man is clearly – if sparsely – indicated on the pre-Viking memorial stones, both by inscriptions and in minor ornamental detail. There has been a tendency – coloured to some extent by later nationalist sentiment – to neglect the possibility of English influence throughout the first millennium. However, perhaps the most important result of recent studies is the demonstration that highly-ornamented sculpture of the pre-Viking period is rare – almost non-existent – in Man. The traditional Manx view that there is much 'Celtic' art in the Island must now be seriously qualified; much of it in reality belongs to the Viking Age and is based on Scandinavian motifs.

The Viking Age

The Viking Age in the west is almost universally accepted as starting symbolically in 793 with a destructive raid on the rich and numinous monastery of Lindisfarne, on Holy Island off the east coast of Northumberland, by 'pagan men'. Its end is less easily defined, but for most purposes a date in the middle of the eleventh century is accepted and is used in this book. The story of the Viking Age, however, is complicated, and the events unravelled by the Vikings in the wider world during this period encompassed not only raiding and warfare, but also political stability, the foundation of towns, active

---

15 Wilson 2008.

CHAPTER 1

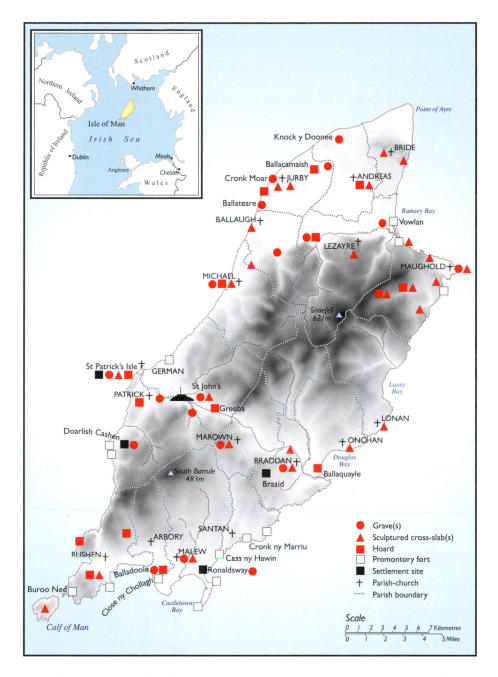

Fig. 4. The Isle of Man in the Viking-age. Major sites mentioned in the text are labelled. The ancient parish-churches and parish boundaries are marked for orientation. The locating map shows important Irish-Sea trading sites of the Viking Age.

international trade, technical innovation, the discovery of new lands by men from Scandinavia, and much more. The events which took place in the Isle of Man form a small part of a story that spreads from the great rivers of Russia, which controlled the trade-routes to the Orient, to the north-east coast of Canada; from Greenland to Spain and the Mediterranean.

The Isle of Man was strategically placed to take its part in these great events. At one time or another Vikings in the west controlled England, western and northern Scotland, Orkney and Shetland, and important enclaves in Ireland and Wales. The Irish Sea became in effect a Viking sea for much of the tenth and eleventh centuries. Through it passed much of the north/south trade of the western littoral of Europe, from Norway and the lands of the North Atlantic, while fleets belonging to various rulers from Norway, the Northern Isles, the Isle of Man, Dublin and York fought to control it politically and economically.

Tracing the history of the Viking Age in the Isle of Man is no simple matter. Evidence for the Viking Age in the Island depends chiefly on archaeology, numismatics, place-names and epigraphy; the most important of these being archaeology. Indeed, the Isle of Man provides the most diverse assemblage of Viking-age archaeology in Britain, comprising settlement sites, fortifications, graves, stone sculpture (with its associated inscriptions), coins and hoards (fig. 4). Contemporary written sources, apart from a number of inscriptions on memorial stones, are brief, tenuous, sometimes corrupt, and difficult to use. The main English sources, which are the most coherent survivals of the period, make no mention of the Isle of Man in the first half of the tenth century, when political and military comings and goings across the Irish Sea, between the sometimes Scandinavian polities of York and Dublin, for example, were at high tension. The sources that do survive have various origins – Irish annals, English chronicles, Welsh histories and Norse sagas. Many were written down long after the events which they record, and are only incidentally concerned with the Island. Conclusions drawn from these sources are often uncritical and over-inflated.

One of the few generally reliable contemporary sources for the Viking Age is the *Anglo-Saxon Chronicle*. Although the Island is never mentioned in it, it does record, under the entry for 973 (well into the Viking Age), how King Edgar of England took his whole fleet to Chester, 'and six kings met him there and pledged their alliance on sea and land'. This entry was expanded more than a hundred years later by Florence of Worcester in his *History of the kings of England*. Using sources now lost, he described the event in greater detail:

> ...and his eight sub-kings, namely Kenneth, king of the Scots, Malcolm, king of the
> Cumbrians, Maccus, king of many islands, and five others, Dufnall, Siferth, Hywel, Jacob,
> and Juchill, met him, as he commanded, and swore that they would be faithful to him
> and be his allies by land and sea.

'Maccus [or Magnus], king of many islands' (described in another twelfth-century source as *archipiratam* – 'chief of the pirates'), may be identified as a king of Man; while the 'many islands' presumably refers to the Island and the Southern Hebrides, a polity mentioned elsewhere in Irish and Welsh annals. This is presumably the polity recorded in later Norse sources (where Man is included with the Hebrides) as the *Suðreyjar* ('the southern isles'), equivalent to 'Man and the Isles' of the later Manx *Chronicle*, and 'Sodor and Man' of the present bishopric.

The fact that this Norse chief – if he really was king of Man and the Isles – was paying homage to an English king is relevant to the turbulent political situation in the Irish Sea at this period; but there is no other tenth-century record of a connection, political or otherwise, between England and Man. Nor is there any record of any raid or other activity in the Island in the first century of the Vikings' appearance in the West. The earliest mention, *c.* 900, is of doubtful validity. This occurs in *Orkneyinga saga,* which was largely compiled *c.*1200, and records a major expedition by Harald Finehair, a Norwegian king. Mentions in other sources – Welsh and Irish – are equally unreliable. One thirteenth-century source suggests that Man was incorporated into the Orkney earldom by 989, although it later established closer connections with Dublin.

It is difficult to say when the Scandinavians first arrived in the Island – there is no written record. The period of raiding, which we know from the written record began in England in 793, started at more or less the same time in Ireland – on Rathlin Island, Co. Antrim – in 794. The most holy monastery of Iona off Mull, reputedly founded by St Columba, was raided in 795 and again in 802 and 806. The latter attacks were so serious that they resulted in the foundation in 807 of a new Columban monastery in Ireland, at Kells, Co. Meath. No definite physical trace of Viking raids has been found in those places where we know them to have been active in this early period, and certainly none in the Isle of Man. The best physical evidence for this initial period of raids in the British Isles is to be found in Norway, where many early Viking-age burials have been found to include insular metalwork, some of which must have been loot – although some was certainly the product of gift-exchange or trade.[16]

It would be inconceivable that the raiders, who were working down the east coast of Ireland – where they ultimately established a series of fortified sites ('*longphoirt*'), of which the most important was Dublin, founded in 841[17] – would have overlooked Man as they sailed southwards through the Northern and Western Isles of Scotland to the Irish Sea to raid in Ireland and Wales. Initially, the Scandinavians came south and west, to pillage rich monasteries (not for religious reasons, but because they were accessible and undefended depositories of wealth and produce), and return home with

16 Wamers 1985.
17 For the latest archaeological evidence concerning the *longphort* at Dublin, see Simpson
    2004.

what portable wealth they could find. Whether there was sufficient movable wealth to interest them on the Island is unknown and unlikely, but (initially at least) slaves could presumably be taken and ships provisioned there. The difficulties with tides and currents mentioned above probably protected Man to some extent, but it is quite possible that, after the establishment of the first Norse bases in Ireland as centres of political and military power in the mid-ninth century, Man became a place of interest, but not in terms of settlement, for the Irish Vikings. Certainly, in the eleventh century, as will be shown (p. 120-1), the Isle of Man was a target for invasion from both Norway and Ireland, as the powers in the region attempted to gain control of the North Channel and hence the Atlantic route to Dublin from both north and south.

What is true of the Isle of Man is probably true of the Irish Sea coast of North-West England and North Wales, where evidence for the presence of the Vikings is equally exiguous. Here, however, towards the end of the ninth century, we begin to find written records of a Scandinavian presence, including settlement, from both Ireland (where the Viking elite had been expelled from their stronghold in Dublin *c.* 902) and from central England (the 'Danelaw'). The archaeological evidence for Viking settlement in North-West England is closely related both in date and form to that found in the Isle of Man.

This earliest evidence for a Viking presence (and presumably settlement) in the Island is provided by a substantial number of pagan burials which date to the ninth and tenth century, and which are accompanied by grave-goods in the Scandinavian fashion. To these we must now turn.

CHAPTER 2

The earliest Vikings in Man

Pagan burials

The Vikings settled in the Isle of Man, around the year 900, and have left many traces, some more coherent than others, which tell of their alien presence (fig. 4). Ironically, we learn most about the initial stages of settlement, of the origin of the settlers and of their cultural and religious orientation and economic and social status, from their graves. Belief in a life which survives the grave is common to the human condition. Such beliefs occupied the pagan Scandinavian mind. Death should not be shameful. It was also important that the memory of a dead person should survive death and that the memory should be good in the eyes of their contemporaries and descendants. It is for these reasons that burial ritual often went beyond the simple disposal of the body and basic mourning to reflect the perceived needs of a person after death and the survival of a good reputation.

The Scandinavians, when they first came to Man, were not Christian and had well-established burial rituals. At different periods and in different areas, throughout Scandinavia and in their settlements overseas, they practised both cremation and inhumation, often furnishing the dead person with goods and equipment which had been used by him or her in life. Few undisputed examples of cremation have been excavated in the British Isles, although they have been recorded in the Western Isles of Scotland and in Derbyshire.[1] In the Isle of Man, as in most of the western Viking settlements, the normal method of disposal of the dead was by inhumation.

From the easternmost part of the Scandinavian area of influence, on the River Volga in Russia, an Arab traveller, Ibn Fadlan, has provided the only surviving contemporary written description of a Viking funeral. It dates from about 922 and is full of gory detail, including a description of the sacrificial offering of a female slave to accompany a rich man on his journey to the afterlife. The full description is very detailed, but a short extract provides some flavour of the whole:

> I was told that when their chieftains died one of the least things which was done was cremation. I was therefore greatly interested to find out about this, until I heard one

---

1 Richards 2004, 23-116. For other possible cremation graves see ibid, 98-9. In Scotland the best documented cremation is from Càrn A' Bharraich, Oronsay: Graham-Campbell and Batey 1998, 113-8, although others have been postulated elsewhere, ibid., 144, and Graham-Campbell 2001, 15-16.

day that one of their chief men was dead. They laid him in his grave and roofed it over for ten days while they cut out and made ready his clothes. What they do is this: for a poor man they make a small boat, place him in it and then burn it; but if he is rich, they gather together his wealth and divide it into three – one part for his family, one part to provide clothes for him, and a third part for *nabidh* [a fermented drink], which they drink on the day that the slave woman is killed and burned together with her master… When a chief has died his family asks his slave women and slaves, "Who will die with him?" Then one of them says, "I will". When she has said this there is no backing out … most of those who agree are women slaves…[2]

This passage illustrates the depth of belief in an afterlife and the elaborate nature of such a belief, even if it was recorded many miles from the Isle of Man and in a different cultural milieu. The memory of such burials survived until well into the Middle Ages. The thirteenth-century Icelander, Snorri Sturluson, for example records the story that the dead were ordered by Odin, chief of the Norse gods, 'to be burned and their possessions with them … that everyone should arrive in Valhalla with such wealth as he had with him on his pyre …'[3]

Old Norse written sources provide a considerable corpus of material about the gods and mythology of early Scandinavia, and of the Vikings' attitudes and beliefs about death and the afterlife. The sources tell of a shadowy underworld ruled by the goddess Hel; but, more familiarly, they also tell of a glorious, heroic and rather bibulous life for fallen warriors in Odin's hall, Valhalla. They tell of contrasting ideas of death, and of funerals and funeral orations. But the reconciliation of such sources, written down some two or three centuries after the conversion of the pagan north to Christianity, with the physical actuality revealed by archaeology is difficult. It is common sense to interpret grave-finds as material of use to the dead in an after life. There is surely also an element of 'impressing the neighbours' and also of indicating to the gods the status of the dead person. Some have tried to read into the cremation rite a need to release the soul or purify the body by fire, even to destroy the memory of a bad death or bad person. But in reality it is now impossible to read concrete meaning into the different techniques of disposal of the Viking dead, particularly as there seem to be no significant differences of geographical distribution. Universal, however, is the gradual cessation of accompanied burial with the coming of Christianity.

Viking graves in the Isle of Man

No example of cremated human remains has been found in Viking-age contexts in the Island (although, as will be shown, burnt animal bones formed part of the burial

---

2 For full translation see Foote and Wilson, 1970 408-11.
3 *Ynglingsaga*, viii.

ritual on more than one site). When the Vikings arrived they were pagans and practised accompanied burial in the manner of their contemporaries in their original homeland. This is not to say that the people who were placed in the graves were not Christian, but the pagan rite may have been used by pagans to hide the actual beliefs of the dead person, to express their own beliefs, or even to take out an 'insurance' in case the new religion did not work. Some twenty-four pagan, or semi-pagan, Norse burial sites in the Isle of Man (fig. 4) represent settlers who were as yet unconverted to Christianity or on the cusp of conversion.[4] All are inhumation burials, and they form two main groups: single burials in mounds, and flat burials, sometimes in pre-existing Christian cemeteries. A third type of burial – a memorial cenotaph without a body – has been proposed for a group of Viking weapons found at Claghbane, Ramsey, although this interpretation must be questioned.[5] The earliest of this group of pagan burials are probably to be dated to the earliest years of the tenth century and the pagan rite was probably practised for at least a generation.

Mound burials

Four Viking-age burials in mounds have been excavated – at Ballateare, Cronk Moar and Ballachrink, all in Jurby, and at Knock y Doonee in the neighbouring parish of Andreas. A fifth grave – a boat-burial at Balladoole, Arbory – is clearly related to this series, it may also originally have been covered by a mound; it was set in a prominent place above what was historically a major farm and was surrounded by a kerb of stones. All were male burials. There is also a record of a skeleton and an axe being found c.1850 in a mound at Ballelby, Patrick, but the finds are lost and the record is poor,[6] whilst there is a distinct possibility that another grave, from Ballaugh, which produced a sword probably made in England, was also in a mound-burial.[7] Other possibilities include Cronk yn How, Lezayre, (p. 38) and Ballachrink (found c.1880, which produced a sword, spearhead and 'a perforated stone disc'),[8] and an unexcavated mound in Jurby churchyard (fig. 5). The graves at Ballateare, Cronk Moar and Balladoole were all excavated in the 1940s by Gerhard Bersu, a brilliant excavator of international reputation, and revealed a great deal more information about the people who lived in the Island in the Viking Age. Knock y Doonee, Andreas, found in 1927, which produced rivets (indicating that it was almost certainly a boat-burial), a sword of Scandinavian

---

4 Exact numbers are difficult to estimate precisely, but see Wilson 1974, 18-29; Cubbon 1983, 16-18; Freke 2002, 83-98; Wilson 2008a.
5 Cubbon 1978-80.
6 Oswald 1860, 77-8.
7 Wilson 2008a.
8 Megaw 1935-7, 234-5 and pl. 116, 2 and 3.

Fig. 5. Probable Viking burial-mound in Jurby churchyard.

type, a spearhead, shield-boss, tools, a ring-pin and horse trappings,[9] was excavated in a less than satisfactory fashion.

Ballateare

Of these the Ballateare burial is perhaps the most revealing of the Viking graves in the Island, because it was the most completely preserved, and produced a wide array of material, as well as evidence of complicated ritual.[10] In the disused yard of the old quarterland farm previously known as Killane,[11] the mound (fig. 6) survived to a height of some 3m and was roughly 12m in diameter. Immediately below the turf which sealed the mound was a layer of cremated animal bones (ox, horse, sheep and dog were identified), in the upper level of the mound could be seen the profile of a central post-hole, probably the remains of a grave-marker. The uppermost layer, which probably represents a sacrificial deposit,[12] covered the much-decayed skeleton of a female between the ages of 20 and 30. At the back of her skull (fig. 7) was a clean-cut sliced hole which was probably the cause of death.[13] This surely represents a human

---

9 Kermode 1930. The plan of the boat in this publication, fig. 1, was reconstructed in the Manx Museum after excavation.

10 Bersu and Wilson 1966, 45-62.

11 For quarterlands, see below, p. 90-2.

12 Unburnt animal bones occur in a number of Scandinavian graves, e.g. grave 3 at Stengade, Langeland, Denmark, Brøndsted 1936, 154-5. The presence of dog among the burnt bones at Ballateare probably precludes its interpretation as a ritual feast.

13 Bersu and Wilson 1966, 48 and pl. XA.

CHAPTER 2

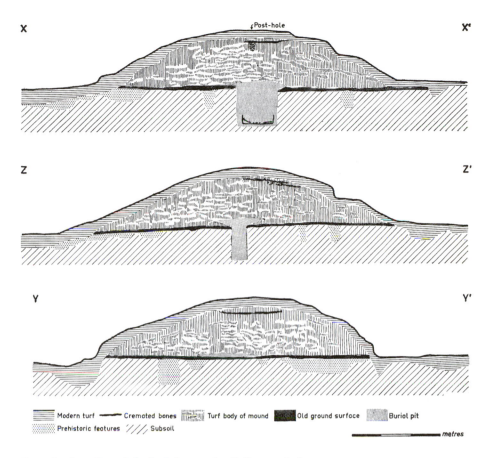

X   Post-hole   X'

Z   Z'

Y   Y'

| ▬▬ Modern turf | ▬▬ Cremated bones | ▦ Turf body of mound | ■ Old ground surface | ▒ Burial pit |
| ░ Prehistoric features | ⁄⁄⁄ Subsoil | | | metres |

Fig. 6. Sections through the burial-mound at Ballateare, Jurby.

sacrifice, a rite familiar to – but rarely found in – the Viking world, and otherwise unknown in the British Isles, although remains at Balladoole (below, p. 39) might represent another. The mound was built of sods stripped from an area of some $500m^2$. The sods were layered horizontally, each being about 20cm thick. The old turf line remained below the mound, save in the area of a burial pit (1.2m deep below the old ground surface), in which had been placed a wooden coffin or wood-lined grave.

The coffin (or cist), which was constructed without nails, contained the body of a man with his head to the west (fig. 8). His skeleton was much decayed, but his teeth tell us that he was aged between 18 and 30.[14] Placed in the grave with him were weapons and a number of other objects. Two spears were laid on top of the coffin, and the shield, with its hemispherical, flanged boss was also placed outside the coffin. Unusually, fragments of the painted white gesso surface of the shield board survive. The colours, which can

14 Lunt 1989-91.

Fig. 7. Top of female skull from Ballateare, showing death-blow.

no longer be seen, were striped in a sequence of alternate black and white bands, with a row of red dots on two of the black bands.[15] The boss (fig. 9) bears the marks of two hefty parallel blows, presumably symbolic of ritual 'killing' before deposition.[16] A sword (fig. 10) seems to have been placed inside the coffin. This, in its scabbard, was hacked into pieces before burial (presumably also a ritual 'killing').[17] The pommel and guard were decorated with inlaid copper and silver wire in geometrical patterns; the sword's form and decoration are Scandinavian. It was probably made in Norway.[18] The leather scabbard was given rigidity by means of two slats of wood and lined with a closely woven woollen cloth. A buckle and strap-mount on the scabbard, together with other mounts, including a strap-end of insular form (i.e. made in the British Isles) belong to the sling for the sword, of which traces survive.[19] A third spearhead was found in the grave, as was a knife with the remains of a wooden handle and a leather sheath.

Study of the man-made objects in the grave opens a window onto the cross-currents of the various cultures which flourished in the Irish Sea in the Viking Age. The sword and one spearhead (with a socket decorated with inlaid copper wire)[20] are of undoubted

---

15 Bersu and Wilson 1966, fig. 37.

16 From a published picture of a male grave at Westness, Rousay, Orkney (an important, largely unpublished site), it would appear that a similarly 'killed' shield boss was excavated there. Owen 2004, fig. 6.

17 The damage to the shield and sword are usually explained as the result of ritual. It is also possible that they were so treated to prevent their recovery by grave-robbers.

18 Petersen 1919, type U; cf. Peirce 2002, 110-4. The sword is described and discussed in detail by Bersu and Wilson 1966, 51-4, fig. 33 and pls. x – xii. A close parallel is from grave 544 at Birka which has a similar pattern of inlay, Arbman 1940, pl. 5.1.

19 Bersu and Wilson 1966, fig. 34.

20 Bersu and Wilson 1960, pl. XIID.

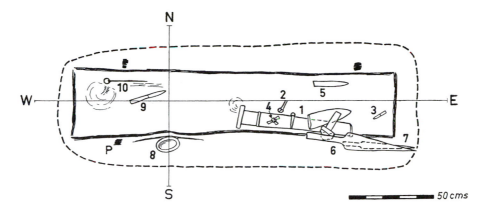

Fig. 8. Grave below the mound, Ballateare.

Norwegian type. The other two spearheads were probably made in the Irish Sea region; parallels being found in the early Viking cemetery at Islandbridge, just outside Dublin.[21] The shield-boss is of a general Scandinavian hemispherical type and could have been made anywhere.[22] The mounts on the scabbard and baldric are also almost certainly of insular – possibly Anglo-Saxon – manufacture, which might imply that the scabbard was also made in the British Isles. All these objects, together with the Irish pin, reflect the cultural and population mix in the Irish Sea region in the early ninth century.

But it is the burial ritual which most closely fits the Scandinavian mode. Few Viking burial-mounds anywhere have revealed so much about the pagan ceremony surrounding the death of a man. It is worth tracing the whole process. First, the burial pit was dug and the body was laid out in a coffin or cist. The man had presumably been dressed in a woollen cloak fastened with a ring-headed pin (fig. 11), also seen at Cronk Moar, (below p. 36). The position of the knife (a multi-purpose implement, equivalent perhaps to the modern army knife) on his chest suggests that it was in a sheath on a belt. His sword, in its scabbard with attached baldric lay by his side and was broken ritually into at least two and possibly three, pieces; its position in the bottom right side of the coffin suggests that it had not been slung round the dead man's shoulder. The third spear was placed inside the coffin; it had either been ritually broken or was little more than 1.5m long. The two spears found outside the coffin were presumably unbroken and had longer shafts (up to 2m). Conditions for the preservation of organic material within the grave were far from ideal, and it is impossible to say whether such things as food and wooden tools and vessels were also placed in the grave, as was sometimes

---

21 Bøe 1940, fig. 10. See Bersu and Wilson 1966, 57; Harrison 2005, 336.
22 Cf. Rygh 1885, fig. 562-3.

Fig. 9. Shield-boss, Ballateare. Showing two slash marks, signs of ritual 'killing'. Diam. 13 cm.

the case elsewhere in the Viking world. It is not clear at what stage the coffin had been lowered into the pit; but, once the external weapons were in place, the pit was backfilled with fine white sand to a level higher than the old ground-surface.

A mound of cut turves was then raised to a height of 1.2m above the in-filled grave, the turf having been cut at some distance from the footprint of the mound. A dead woman was then laid in the upper levels of this turf mound. The top of her head had been cut off (fig. 7) and rigor mortis had already set in – her arms were in a raised position – demonstrating that she had been killed between twelve and seventy-two hours before the mound was completed. A substantial post was then raised in the middle of the top of the mound and its socket was packed with stones. The whole was then completed with a substantial deposit of black earth covering a significant layer of burnt animal bones some 7-8cm thick; the whole was then presumably capped with a layer of sods.

The most interesting feature of the Ballateare burial is the element of sacrificial offering, most strikingly shown by the woman who was almost certainly killed in order

Fig. 10. Sword with hilt inlaid with copper and silver. Ballateare.

to accompany the dead man to the afterlife. This reflects the description of the ritual sacrifice described by Ibn Fadlan in the passage quoted above. One may assume, as was the case on the Volga, that the Ballateare woman was a slave, valued on the same scale as the animals which had clearly been burnt as an offering. The unceremonious nature of the disposal of the woman's body, without a coffin and in a condition of rigor mortis, demonstrates how little she was regarded in death.

Slavery was common at this period, not only in the Viking world, but also in most of the neighbouring Christian countries (see below p. 89). Presumed slaves – male and female – buried with their master or mistress are encountered elsewhere in the Viking world and are also mentioned in later literary sources.[23] It must be stressed that many ordinary double burials – graves containing both men and women – are simply that (husband and wife, for example), and provide evidence neither of suttee nor of

---

23 Jesch 1991, 24-7.

sacrificed slaves. On the other hand, it is highly probable that a slave was buried in the rich ship-burial at Oseberg in Norway, which clearly had a similar, if far grander, ritual than that at Ballateare.[24] A rather more problematic rich burial is a tenth-century boat-grave at the international market-place at Kaupang, Vestfold, Norway, which contained the bodies of a man and two women, as well as of a horse.[25] This has been seen as the burial of a husband and wife, accompanied by a woman, with trans-sexual grave-goods, who has been interpreted as a sorceress. Whether she was sacrificed or not is open to question.

A number of double graves in south Scandinavia provide slightly ambivalent evidence of ceremonial sacrifice, in that the head of the second person in the grave has been deliberately separated from the body.[26] On the other hand, in most such cases, the grave-goods are rarely as rich as at Ballateare, and are often so slight that one wonders whether there is another explanation for the second body – a man executed for murder or rape and buried with his victim, for example. Such could be the case at Gerdrup, Sjælland, Denmark, where a man, bound hand and foot, having a broken neck, was buried with a woman furnished with a spear and knife, overlaid by two large stones.[27] This is a strange grave; the spear – a male weapon – is not normally found in a woman's grave;[28] further, the executed man was laid in a chamber built for two bodies – only paralleled in Denmark at Stengade, Langeland, where both bodies were male.[29]

It has been suggested above that the Ballateare sword and shield (and almost certainly one of the spearheads), had been deliberately broken or damaged before being placed in the grave – examples of a sacrificial ritual of a kind found elsewhere in Viking-age Scandinavian graves, and indeed in graves of earlier periods. The animal-bones (whether the remains of cremated animals or burnt offerings of meat dishes) are another sacrificial element in the grave, reflecting an earlier Germanic ritual encountered, for example, in Anglo-Saxon graves in England.[30] Other such deposits represent the remains of

---

24 Brøgger 1917, 146-50; Christensen 1992, 40-1.
25 Skre 2007, 95-9, fig. 5.20.
26 Roesdahl 1980, 27, 189, fig. 7.
27 Christensen 1981; Christenesen and Bennike 1983. Some graves are even more difficult to interpret, e.g. grave 1 from Lockarp, Skåne, Sweden, Svanberg 2003, 290, might represent a sacrifice, but might also have contained more than one body laid down at a later date, of which one had his head between his legs. Svanberg's statement, p. 87, that human sacrifice was, 'relatively common in south-west Scania', is difficult to sustain on the basis of the evidence presented.
28 Figures, arguably women, possibly sorceresses (Price 2003, 169ff), are depicted carrying a spear on the Oseberg embroideries, Christensen 1981, 186; Christensen and Nockert 2006, figs.1-26, 54, but see ibid. fig. 100.
29 Skaarup 1976, 56-8.
30 E.g. Carver 2005, 279-80.

CHAPTER 2

Fig. 11. Cloak-pin. Ballateare. Scale 1:1.

funerary feasts – and this is a possibility at Ballateare, although the sacrificial element is emphasised in the way in which the burnt bones were spread over the top of the mound (and by the fact that dog is generally taboo as food in western cultures). The turf used in the construction of the mound may even also have had some sacrificial status, representing perhaps the land owned by the dead man.

The date of the objects suggests that this could be the grave of one of the first Viking land-takers in Man in the late ninth or early tenth century. It was clearly the burial of a rich man. The labour of constructing the mound alone implies a considerable outlay, while the grave-goods and sacrificial deposit represent an offering of great value. The post raised above the mound may have carried some symbol of his status, but the permanency of the structure and the ritual which would have been observed by his contemporaries were intended to emphasise that the grave, and the mound which it covered, was the memorial to an esteemed man, presumably a landowner buried on his own land. The mound was also a statement in the landscape, a symbol of power. What is more, the people who buried him were making a religious statement, perhaps even one of religious propaganda, emphasising their belief in an after-life in Valhalla, in a period when such beliefs were being challenged by Christianity. Such an emphasis – almost aggressive – has been noted in Denmark, when the country was on the cusp of the acceptance of Christianity. At the royal site of Jelling, in Jutland, the dying years of pagandom produced one of the grandest burial-mounds of the Viking Age, a statement not only of the importance of the person buried there but also of support for contemporary pagan religion at the period of its greatest challenge.[31] This emphasis on the buried man's status, as at Jelling, and the claims of the incomer at Ballateare were enhanced by the position of the mound in the landscape. Although it is today difficult to appreciate the appearance of the Viking-age landscape, the placing of this mound and others in Man on ridges or eminences demonstrates that here, as elsewhere in the Germanic world, they were positioned for

31 E.g. Roesdahl 1993, 132.

Fig. 12. Spear-head from Cronk Moar, Jurby. Length: 52cm.

maximum effect – an advertisement of religion, prestige and power; in this case signalling the establishment of a new order.[32]

Cronk Moar

Closest in form and content to Ballateare was the mound-burial at Cronk Moar, some 1.5km from Ballateare, About 30m from the edge of a high cliff, the mound was removed in 1939 (to make way for the construction of a watch-tower for a bombing range). The mound was recorded by Ifor Bowen,[33] who noted no details of its construction. He did, however, find within it fragments of burnt material – clay, bone, teeth and shells – as well as a few fragments of nails and other pieces of unidentifiable iron, a layer which might parallel the cremated material encountered at Ballateare. The site was sealed after its removal, and Bersu completed the excavation in 1945. The mound covered an area of about 60m² and had been built directly on the old ground surface, which still bore traces of Viking-age ploughing. The burial pit, in the middle of the area covered by the mound contained what was either a wood-lined cist or a coffin of oak. Above the 'coffin', and protruding over its edge, was a spearhead. Within it were the very decayed and fragmentary remains of a man's skeleton. He was dressed in a woollen cloak fastened by a ring-headed cloak-pin of Irish form, of a type commonly found in the western areas of Viking settlement of the British Isles.[34]. The cloak was made of a pile-weave cloth (Old Norse *rǫgg*), which is constructed by laying short lengths of wool in the shed (i.e. placing them or tying them round the warp threads during weaving). When finished the short lengths of wool appear as tufts and the cloth produced has a shaggy appearance. Such textiles are found elsewhere in Scandinavian settlements at home and overseas.[35] Accompanying the burial was a much corroded sword of Scandinavian type in its scabbard, the guard being inlaid with wire of either copper alloy or silver in a manner similar to that found at Ballateare.[36] The scabbard, which was of similar construction to that from Ballateare, was covered with moulded leather

---

32 Cf. Roesdahl 1997; Roesdahl 2005.
33 Bersu and Wilson 1966, 63-83.
34 For this and other pins in Manx graves see Fanning 1983. See also Fanning 1994, fig. 11.
35 Bersu and Wilson 1966, fig. 47. Ewing 2006, 145-6.
36 Ibid., figs. 41 and 42, pl. XIIB. Probably a variant of Petersen 1919, type U (especially figs. 122-3), cf. Peirce 2002, 110-1. It is very similar to the Ballateare sword.

CHAPTER 2

Fig. 13. The restored burial-mound at Knock y Doonee, Andreas.

and was attached to a baldric by means of a buckle and other mounts. The spearhead (fig. 12) is probably of insular type. The conical shield-boss was of a normal Irish Sea form.[37] A knife completes the grave inventory.

The parallels between the Ballateare and Cronk Moar graves are striking, not only in the form of the burial and the use of a coffin or wood-lined cist, but also in the grave-goods and the presence of what may be sacrificial cremated animals and a 'killed' sword which, as at Ballateare, is broken into three pieces. The general furnishing of the two graves is very similar, even the sword-slings can be closely compared. Further, the size of the mounds and their situation in the landscape are very similar. The two graves must be closely related in date.

Knock y Doonee and other mound-burials

The much larger burial-mound at Knock y Doonee (fig. 13) was excavated with a great deal less skill in the late 1920s.[38] 17m in diameter and at least 2.3m high, like Ballateare and Cronk Moar it makes a statement in the landscape. A series of clench-nails found in the base of the mound suggest that the dead man was buried in a small boat. In the grave were a Scandinavian-type sword,[39] a spearhead, a fragment of a hemispherical shield-boss of typical Scandinavian type, knife smith's tools (metal-shears and a hammer), a lead fishing-line sinker and other items, including a horse-harness with mounts of a form found elsewhere in the Irish Sea region (including the Balladoole burial – see below) and a horse. Horses are well-known accessories in graves of this period throughout the Viking world: the really rich being accompanied by a number of horses – some twelve were buried with the great Norwegian Gokstad ship,[40] and

---

37 Harrison 2000, 68-70.
38 Kermode 1930.
39 Probably Petersen 1919, type U. It has traces of ?silver wire encrustation on the guard.
40 Nicolaysen 1882, 52.

fifteen – all decapitated – with the Oseberg vessel;[41] more normally a single horse is found, as in Grave 3 at Stengade, Langeland, Denmark – where the animal had been killed by a blow to the frontal bone as it stood in the grave-pit.[42]

There is a handful of other burial-mounds of the Viking Age in the Island. But there are also many mounds which cannot, without excavation, be dated. An intriguing example, which (because of the modern burials which cover it) has not been excavated, is the mound in the graveyard of Jurby parish church (pl. 5), less than a kilometre from Cronk Moar. There is no evidence that this is of Viking-age date, but it is likely. Viking burials (see below p. 51) in a number of Island churchyards are indicated by finds of weapons (chiefly such easily recognisable objects as swords) – a phenomenon well known elsewhere in the British Isles. It is an intriguing possibility that the Jurby mound, like the royal mounds at Jelling in Denmark,[43] formed the focus of the Christian graveyard of the later parish church.

Another possible mound-burial was excavated at Cronk yn How, Lezayre.[44] It is exceedingly difficult to interpret. At the lowest level of the site is a cemetery made up of burials in stone-lined grave pits (in the Island known as 'lintel-graves'). This was overlain by a layer of burnt earth and the remains of a mound. Traces of its ditch survived. The mound, which would have had a prominent position in the landscape, appears to have been cut into by a later rectangular building, presumably a keeill. In the layer above the lintel-graves are scattered artefacts of Viking type, including hinges and about sixty clench-nails and roves which presumably formed part of a 60cm-long substantial wooden strong-box. Also found was a glass bead of Viking type, a spindle-whorl and a sickle. These objects probably came from a woman's grave.

The Balladoole burial

A Viking burial placed on the most prominent part of an earlier Christian cemetery, itself set within a prehistoric enclosure (fig. 14), was excavated by Bersu at Balladoole, Arbory.[45] It is arguably much richer than those found at Ballateare, Cronk Moar or Knock y Doonee, but is of similar date. The body of a man was laid in a clinker-built oak boat, some 11m in length (fig. 15), set within a kerb of large stones, the whole of which was capped by smaller stones, and was probably covered by a mound of earth (since eroded away). The burial disturbed a number of lintel-graves which (as at Cronk yn How) formed part of a small pre-existing Christian cemetery (fig. 16). This superimposition

---

41 Brøgger 1917, 145-6.
42 Brøndsted 1936, 154 and fig. 65.
43 See Pedersen 2006, for a thorough discussion of mound-burials in Denmark.
44 Bruce and Cubbon 1930.
45 Bersu and Wilson 1966, 1-44. See also Müller-Wille 2002.

Fig. 14. The enclosure on Chapel Hill, Balladoole, Arbory. The boat burial, outlined by stones, lies on the bank, bottom left. The later keeill is at the top of the picture.

complicates the story as traces of at least three individuals (there were three skulls) were found in the grave, of which only two skulls were reasonably complete. There can be little doubt that the boat-grave was constructed for a male, whose substantial skeleton was excavated. The disturbance of the underlying graves during the construction of the boat-grave and its cairn, and subsequent depredations by rabbits, suggest that the extra bones were the disturbed remains of pre-existing burials. It is, however, conceivable that this was a double burial. As, however, there were no specifically female grave-goods in the deposit, it is conceivable that some of the bones represent the sacrificial remains of a slave, like that found at Ballateare.

The only weapon found in the grave was a shield (fig. 17), represented by its grip and a conical boss of a type found mostly in the Western Isles and Ireland.[46] The man had two or three knives, a hone, a flint strike-a-light, a belt (represented by a buckle with a cast loop and a strap-end) and a ring-headed pin of Irish type, not dissimilar to that found at Ballateare, to fasten his cloak. Traces of linen were presumably part of a shirt.

---

46 Harrison 2000, 68-70.

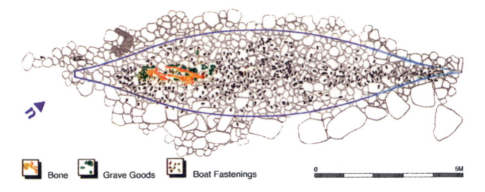

Bone   Grave Goods   Boat Fastenings

0   5M

Fig. 15. The boat-burial at Balladoole. The rivets and nails are all that is left of the boat. The reconstructed outline of the boat is shown as a blue line. (Drawing by Tony Daly after Redknap 2000.)

Fig. 16. Balladoole. Kerb of boat-burial overlying the earlier lintel-graves.

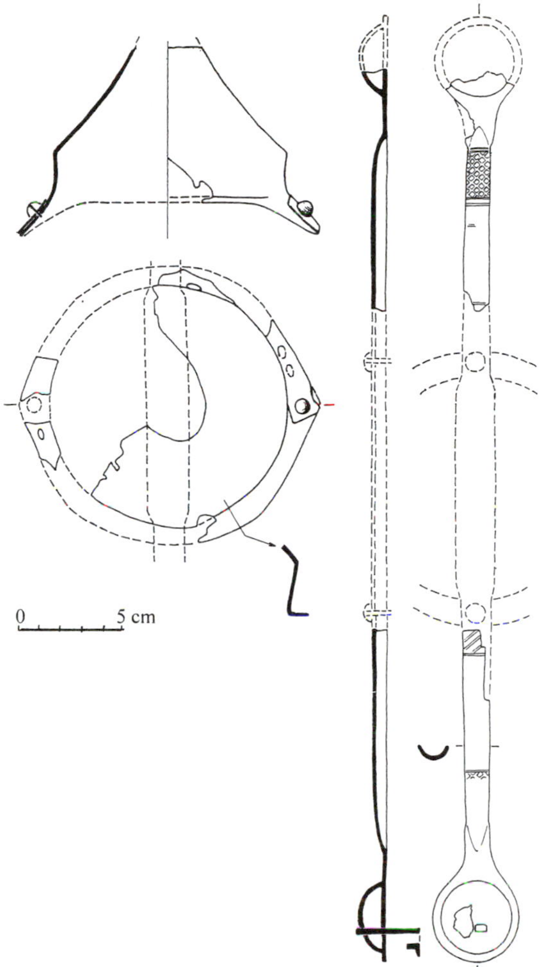

Fig. 17. Shield-boss and grip from Balladoole.

0   5 cm

The grave-goods also included the iron handle of a bucket (presumably made of some perishable organic material such as leather or wood), a silver-gilt buckle and strap-end, decorated bridle-mounts of sheet bronze (fig. 18) with a single-jointed iron snaffle-bit, a pair of iron spurs and associated cast copper-alloy buckles (fig. 18), strap-slides and strap-ends, stirrup-irons (fig. 19) and iron loops for stirrup-leathers (probably all that remains of a complete saddle).

     Of particular interest is the riding equipment with its hint of luxury and the exotic, clearly the property of a man of high status. Only the rich could afford horses, and horses, therefore, were presumably uncommon on the Island. The equipment consists of a bridle and the remains of a saddle, with a pair of up-to-date – perhaps exotic – stirrups, as well as a pair of spurs and their associated buckles and mounts. The bridle was almost

Fig. 18. Bridle- and strap-mounts from the Balladoole burial. Top, bronze mounts from the bridle; below, silver-gilt buckle and strap-end from a belt; bottom, gilt-bronze strap-slide and strap-end from a spur. Scale 1:1.

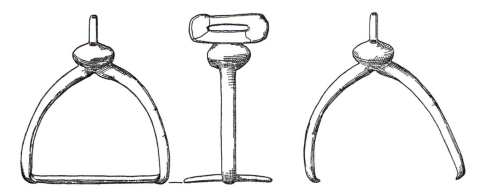

Fig. 19. Iron stirrup-irons from Balladoole. Scale approx. 1:3.

certainly made in Ireland, probably at Dublin,[47] or at least in the Irish Sea region, for the engraved sheet-bronze mounts and buckles which embellished it are paralleled not only at Knock y Doonee[48] and St. Patrick's Isle,[49] but in the Western Isles in a boat-burial at Kiloran Bay, Colonsay,[50] as well as in the excavations of Viking-age Dublin.[51]

The other pieces of riding equipment are also interesting. The Balladoole stirrup-irons (fig. 19) are unlike most of those found in Scandinavia, which are much longer and mostly of slightly later date.[52] They are amongst the earliest found in the British Isles and are most closely paralleled by examples in France and Moravia (stirrups seem to have been introduced into Western Europe in the late seventh century).[53] The cast buckles and mounts which form a set with the spurs (which themselves are very different from Scandinavian types) are also exotic and come either from the south of England or, as is more likely, from the Carolingian empire, as did the silver buckle and strap-end. These objects are intrinsically important in themselves, for ornamented objects of such an origin are rarely found in the British Isles. Interestingly, however, mounts of similar type were found just across the water in a female grave at Claughton Hall, Lancashire, and in the now lost material from the Viking-age burial-mound at Aspatria, Cumbria.[54] Both finds come from an area which had close contacts with Man in the Viking Age. A further indication of the status of the burial is the quality of a minute portion of what was presumably part of the dead man's shirt; it was made of an exceptionally fine linen which had a thread count of 28 × 32 per cm, more than

47 Some of the buckles are dealt with in Paterson 2001, especially p. 131.
48 Kermode 1930, fig. 3.
49 Freke 2002, fig. 25.
50 Grieg 1940, fig. 30.
51 Ó Riordáin 1976, pl. 17.
52 Pedersen 1997 and 2002; Petersen 1951, 32-6.
53 Bersu and Wilson 1966, 30-1.
54 Edwards, B. J. N. 1992, fig. 5.1.

double normal fineness and only paralleled in the British Isles by a single piece from York.[55]

Graves with riding tackle have been best studied in Denmark – where forty-eight graves have been found – although they occur throughout Scandinavia.[56] In Denmark the form of burial varies, but it is taken as axiomatic that the presence of such equipment (occasionally found, as at Knock y Doonee, with a horse) is indicative of the military status of a dead man as well as of his wealth.[57] At this period, however, battles were not fought on horseback. The horse would enable a warrior to move quickly to threatened trouble, where he could abandon his mount and fight on foot. Although the horse had greater utility in more peaceful contexts, it remained a status symbol. Riding tackle in a grave was not only an indicator of status; it was also, in the context of burial, symbolic of the possibility of travel to, and in, the next world. An analogous symbolism might also account for the presence of cremated horse bones in the capping of the Ballateare grave; it might also be reflected in the depictions of riders on some of the carved memorial stones which are discussed in the next chapter. While it is likely that the men buried in these graves were known as warriors, it would be important, whatever their prowess, that they would have the wherewithal to ride to Valhalla; there to live with Odin and fight with the gods against the powers of chaos as the world comes to an end at Ragnarǫk.

The rite of boat-burial found at Balladoole and Knock y Doonee is not common in the Scandinavian settlements of the British Isles.[58] Others are known from Kiloran Bay[59] and, probably, Machrins,[60] on Colonsay in the southern Hebrides; Scar and Westness, Orkney (where there are two);[61] and possibly one or two at Pierowall, Orkney.[62] A possible cremated boat from Oronsay is mentioned above (p. 25n). All these graves contained the remains of clinker-built rowing-boats of a type found with the great ship-burial at Gokstad, Norway.[63] A substantial number of burials in boats of this size

---

55 Ewing 2006, 142.

56 Lyngstrøm 1993; Pedersen 1997.

57 Roesdahl, 2006, 169-73.

58 A possible third Manx boat-burial is suggested by the find of a handful of clench-nails in the cemetery on St. Patrick's Isle, Wright, 1980-2 36 and fig. 11. Cubbon 1982, 276, records a suggestion of Bersu that the Cronk yn Howe keeill overlay a Viking boat-burial, the original occupant of the grave being given a Christian re-burial. This is almost certainly a misinterpretation of the evidence, see p. 38 above.

59 Anderson 1906-7; Graham-Campbell and Batey 1998, 119-22 *et passim*; Bill 2005. For a distribution-map of Viking-age boat-burials in the British Isles see Müller-Wille 2002, fig. 7.

60 Graham-Campbell and Batey 1998, 90.

61 Owen and Dalland 1999; Graham-Cambell and Batey 1998, 136-8.

62 Ibid., 134.

63 Brøgger and Shetelig 1971, 41.

have been found in Scandinavia, and particularly in Norway.[64] The Manx examples were not, of course, sea-going vessels of the form well-known from the great Viking ships excavated at Oseberg and Gokstad in Norway, or raised from the bed of Roskilde Fjord in Denmark. They were small craft between 5 and 15m long, useful for fishing, for coastwise travel, or as tenders to move people and goods out to bigger vessels anchored off-shore.

A boat in a grave is not merely a symbol of the importance of the dead person (although it is clearly that); as a dead man equipped with horse trappings would be able to ride to the next world, so too he would be able to travel there by boat. The occurrence of both riding equipment and a boat in two Manx burials is reflected in the art of Viking-age Sweden, where boats and riders occur together on what are presumably memorial stones from the Baltic island of Gotland.[65] Towards the beginning of the Viking Age the Gotland stones show ships under sail, often together with mounted men apparently being welcomed to Valhalla by women bearing drinking-horns.[66]

The fact that few – if any – of the grave-goods found at Balladoole were made in Scandinavia is significant. The objects would not be out of place in the burial of any wealthy man in the west of Scandinavia, even down to the occasional piece of exotica (the bridle and other mounts, for example), for imported material from the British Isles is often to be found in Norwegian graves.[67] But the quantity of exotic goods and material made in the Irish Sea region, and the paucity of purely Scandinavian material found in the Manx burial-mounds and at Balladoole, clearly sets these graves apart from those of their Scandinavian contemporaries, and would almost certainly indicate that the men buried here had lived in the region for some time before their death.

The man in the Balladoole boat-burial, although he had apparently lived in the region for some time must, like those in the mound-burials, have been an important first-generation Norse settler in the Island. It has been suggested that the burial, located on the highest point of the hill within a pre-existing Christian cemetery, 'violently rejects' Christian ideology in dramatic fashion.[68] The author of this proposition, S. Tarlow, goes on to write,

---

64 Müller-Wille 1974; for the latest distribution map of boat-burials, Müller-Wille 1995, fig. 2. Boats of similar size occur in Sweden; their significance has recently been discussed by Larsson 2007.

65 Riders and boats also appear separately on late Viking memorial stones throughout Sweden; Fuglesang 2005.

66 Lindqvist 1941.

67 Wamers 1985, 90-106.

68 Tarlow 1997, 139-40. (She seems to have conflated in her description two graves, Balladoole and Ballateare, but this would not affect her argument.)

... this boat burial expresses particular tensions between a small elite group and the rest of the population. These differences were not only acted out in the struggle for symbolic and actual possession of the most prominent position in the landscape, but the graves themselves were the location in which political and ethnic relations were violently expressed.

This interpretation is I believe partly correct. Aggressively placed in the landscape, it was presumably an expression of propaganda for the old religion. I do not, however, believe that the disturbance of the early graves at Balladoole was deliberate in the sense that Tarlow sees it, as an expression of the violent and bloody times in which the land-taking took place. The grave in my view represents at least an acceptance (as elsewhere in the Island) of the sacred nature of the site, while following the pagan burial-rite of Scandinavia. At the same time it symbolised the power and status of the new settler – a wealthy landowner with a background as a warrior. The weapons and horse trappings found, both here and in the mound-burials, show that they were burials of men of wealth and status, a cut above the ordinary warrior with his single weapon buried in a less prominent position.

Cemeteries

It must be stressed that, at the beginning of the Viking Age, there was no such thing as consecrated Christian burial-grounds in the rural areas of north-west Europe. The dead in all rural areas were buried either in a family cemetery (or in a cemetery reserved for the community) by the family itself, probably without assistance from the clergy and in almost every case without benefit of an ecclesiastical building. Gradually this changed, and by the tenth century in much of Anglo-Saxon England, for instance, the presence of the clergy at burials became increasingly obligatory and cemeteries began to be consecrated.[69] In the west, in Cornwall and Wales for example, the old practices continued, and this was certainly the case in the Isle of Man (indeed burial in old unconsecrated cemeteries continued into the nineteenth century). The man buried at Balladoole was presumably buried in the cemetery which had been used by the previous owners of the land and by their families and servants; the Viking incomer thereby emphasising his own legitimacy.

In other parts of the Island a number of Norse weapons (particularly swords) have been discovered during later grave-digging in the cemeteries of the parish churches.[70] These churchyards were presumably formed around family cemeteries when parishes were established in the twelfth century, but most had a demonstrably pre-Viking origin

69 Discussed in Blair 2005, 463-6.
70 Listed in Wilson 1974, 44-5. See map, fig. 4.

as family burial grounds. In a few cases – at Maughold for example – there is evidence of a greater number of burials, in this case presumably in the cemetery of the pre-Viking monastic establishment.

A similar community situation – either lay or clerical – may be seen on St. Patrick's Isle, within the enclosure which later became Peel Castle. Between 1982 and 1987 the remains of some 327 individuals were excavated to the north of the later cathedral, some of which were presumably related to a small but substantially-built tenth- or early eleventh-century keeill (chapel) which was surrounded by burials.[71] Many of the burials found on the islet were in lintel-graves, but some were in coffins and some were placed directly in the earth. They bracketed a period from the sixth to the fourteenth century and, if elementary mathematics is applied to the archaeologically excavated area, the number of burials laid down each year cannot have been many. The question of the character of the islet's community must remain open but in the eleventh century it might (as earlier) have had a monastic character (below p. 127-8).

Eight burials, of which two were infants, were convincingly dated to the first half of the tenth century and, on the basis of the objects found in the graves (including clothes and personal ornaments), they probably represent Scandinavian settlers who had been brought up in a non-Christian Scandinavian tradition. One child's grave was uncoffined and contained a silver halfpenny of the English king Eadred (946-55);[72] the other child's grave was coffined and contained a small bell, six glass and two amber beads.[73] The lintel-grave of an adult male contained a penny of the English king Eadmund (939-46), a copper-alloy ring-headed dress pin of Irish type (related to those found at Balladoole, Ballateare and Cronk Moar) and a buckle with a decorated plate like those found at Balladoole and Knock y Doonee.[74] The body had been wrapped for the grave in a cloak trimmed with at least eighteen woven silver wire tassels, most closely paralleled in a grave in Iceland,[75] but probably not made there. A more likely source might be England or Ireland, where a number of similar trimmings have been found. Traces of silver trimmings were found in another male grave on St. Patrick's Isle.[76] Another burial (probably that of a man) was contained in a curved-lidded chest; with him were a plain ring-headed pin which apparently fastened a linen cloak or shroud. A belt was represented by a strap-end and buckle; traces of a comb and what might be an awl were also found in the grave.[77] Another grave included the remains of a casket,

---

71 Freke 2002.
72 Ibid,, 71, 326-7, and fig. 19.
73 Ibid., 70, 94, 351, figs. 19, 26 and 108.
74 Ibid., 69-70, 87-9, 326, figs. 19, 21, and pl.20.
75 At Kápa á Almenningum, Vestur-Eyjafjallahreppur. For these and other similar tassels see Graham-Campbell 2005, 132-3, and fig. 3.
76 Freke 2002. 71, 89 and fig. 19.
77 Ibid., 70, 91, figs. 19 and 22.

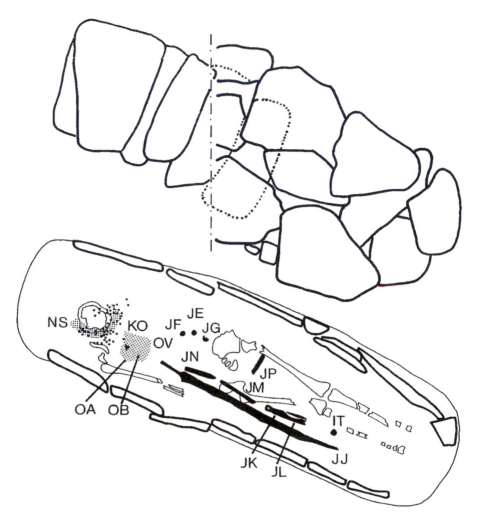

Fig. 20. Plan of woman's grave, St Patrick's Isle. Above, capstones of the lintel-grave. Below, the skeleton and grave-goods: JM, JN knives; JL bone comb; JK iron shears; JJ iron cooking-spit; NS down pillow; the beads (fig. 21) are below the skull. (After Freke 2002.)

a belt-buckle with decorated plate, a strap-end and an iron knife in a mounted leather sheath.[78]

Most important, however, was the richly-furnished grave of a middle-aged woman of high status (the only accurately-sexed tenth-century skeleton found on the site) buried in a lintel-grave of elaborate but normal local type (fig. 20).[79] She wore a woollen dress with a woven sash, and possibly a head-covering. Her head rested on a down-filled

---

78 Ibid., 71, 91-4, figs. 19, 25, and pl. 24.
79 Ibid., 66, 83-7, figs. 19, 20 and pl. 18; Holgate 1987.

48   CHAPTER 2

Fig. 21. Beads from a woman's grave, St Patrick's Isle.

pillow. With her were an iron roasting-spit,[80] the remains of three knives (the grips of two of which were embellished with inlaid silver wire), a pair of shears, an antler comb, two needles, a miniature 'pestle and mortar' (possibly of phallic significance) of limestone and a pierced ammonite. There was also a fine necklace (fig. 21) consisting of seventy-three beads of coloured glass, amber (probably from the Baltic) and jet from Whitby. Traces of textiles were found on the corroded iron of the spit and shears (including three different types of cord) and impressions of feathers from a bird's wing which might have been used for sweeping or basting. Traces of cooking herbs were also recovered. There would be nothing remarkable about this grave if it were found in Norway, save that it contains no specifically Scandinavian objects (other possibly than the spit and the necklace), and no brooches of the type usually found in female Viking graves, although this is presumably merely an indication of a comparatively late date for the burial, towards the second quarter of the tenth century.[81] The pagan nature of the woman's burial, accompanied as she was by grave-goods, suggests that she was an incomer, although it is possible that she was a native Christian buried in pagan fashion by pagan relatives. No other female burial of similar high status has been found on the Island. Further, it should be said that none of the other burials with accompanying

---

80 Price 2003, 160, suggests that this is the staff of a *vǫlva*, a peripatetic seer or sorceress. The length of the object, its form and the other domestic equipment found in the grave make this idea difficult to support, and Price is said to be withdrawing this suggestion.

81 But cf. graves of similar date in Iceland – Eldjárn 1956. 194-384.

grave-goods in the St. Patrick's Isle cemetery have such a strong claim to be recognised as pagan (although more might be found in further excavations on the site).

The material found in the graves on St. Patrick's Isle suggests that these burials belong to the first half of the tenth century and represent the first or second generation of settlers whose relatives used a residual pagan Scandinavian burial rite. They reflect a society of mixed ethnic origin coming to terms with, or at least tolerant of, each other's religious practices, pagan or Christian. There may be some ambiguity about the ethnicity of the people buried here with accompanying grave-goods, but there is little doubt that the ritual was – at least in part – pagan, although they were laid to rest in a pre-existing Christian cemetery, many in stone-lined graves of a form found in earlier times elsewhere on the Island.

In a period of conversion burial ritual is likely to be confused, as it may or may not be influenced by the new religion. A person buried with grave-goods may or may not have been pagan, particularly if these were simply embellishments of the everyday clothes in which the dead person was interred. Similarly, the absence of grave-goods need not mean that the dead person was Christian. The decision of the family after death might be coloured either by belief or by custom, so that some burials cannot be assigned to any particular rite. The rite of unaccompanied burial, in Man as elsewhere, did eventually become the norm, but in effect it could not be restrained or controlled until the clergy took over, often when a church or chapel was built. It is likely, however, that the conversion process was reasonably quick in the Isle of Man (as will be shown in the next chapter) and the ambivalence between accompanied and unaccompanied burial was soon resolved. The few known Scandinavian parallels would suggest that, even when the dead were buried with grave-goods in churchyards, they were at least nominally Christian, for by this time the clergy controlled the funerary ritual.[82]

Only two other graves of women buried in a pagan manner have been found in the Island. One may be represented by a group of beads, found about 1848 in what was probably a lintel-grave a short distance to the west of Tynwald Hill at St. John's,[83] and another by objects found in a mound at Cronk yn How (above p. 38).[84] There were almost certainly graves at the appallingly excavated site at Ronaldsway (below p. 117-8). Many of the objects found there could have been burial goods, indeed a spear-head seems to have been found with the remains of a skeleton and a balance arm (fig. 51) in the lintel cemetery there;[85] but how many objects came from graves on this important site will never be known.

82 E.g. Kieffer-Olsen 2004, 178.
83 Megaw 1937, 237 and pl. 117. Cf. Barnwell 1868, 102-3. See also Oswald 1860, 198.
84 Bruce and Cubbon 1930, figs. 16, 17.
85 Neely 1940, 77, 83.

Viking graves in flat cemeteries – with or without lintel-grave construction – are well evidenced, but one anomalous find deserves mention. In 1937 workmen discovered two graves some 350m south-east of Tynwald Hill, which led to the investigation of a cemetery of 29 lintel-graves.[86] Later a group of weapons was found which were apparently not associated with any of these graves. These appear to be grave-goods of a Norse character – a hemispherical shield-boss of general Scandinavian type, a sword and spearhead, of types found elsewhere on the Island. It has been suggested that this was a memorial burial – a cenotaph like that from Claghbane referred to above (p. 27) – which has been compared to similar possible cenotaphs in Scotland.[87] It may, however, merely represent material thrown out in digging later graves. The Cronk yn How grave mentioned above is one of a number of lintel-graves in cemeteries in the island, the exact status of which is hard to define;[88] but Viking graves do occur – if rarely – in secondary contexts in mounds elsewhere in the British Isles.[89] The objects from this grave – knife, sickle and casket mounts – are easily paralleled in Scandinavia.

Single finds of weapons of Viking-age form from various sites probably come from graves. A convincing case has been made, for example, for a sword found at Ballabrooie, Patrick, to be part of a burial deposit.[90] The same is presumably true of the single finds of Viking-age date (chiefly swords) from ancient graveyards mentioned above, which were still in use until recently – at Kirk Braddan, Malew, Maughold, Jurby and Kirk Michael.[91] These finds, like some of those found in the graves from the continuously-used cemetery on St. Patrick's Isle, probably represent the burials of the first generation of Norse settlers.

Manx graves in context

The commonest rite of Viking burial in the Isle of Man is, then, that of interment in pre-existing Christian flat-grave cemeteries (often in lintel-graves of the native tradition). In Scotland such graves in Christian cemeteries have rarely been found,[92] but more are known from north-west England, where some of the best parallels to material found

---

86 Megaw 1938. Normally referred to as the Balladoyne cemetery (it is in the treen of that name).
87 Graham-Campbell and Batey 1998, 144; see also pp. 96 and 99. For putative English cenotaphs see Richards 2002, 168.
88 Bruce and Cubbon 1930. See also p. 38, above.
89 E.g. the doubtful examples cited by Richards 2002, 158-9.
90 Cubbon 1965.
91 For references see Wilson 1974, 44-5. See also Wilson 2008a.
92 Graham-Campbell and Batey 1998, 144.

in the Manx graves occur.[93] In Ireland there is also – somewhat sparse – evidence of Norse burials in pre-Viking-age cemeteries, at Kilmainham and Donnybrook in Co. Dublin, and possibly at Church Bay, Rathlin Island, Co. Antrim.[94]

Mounds of the size which cover the Manx burials, although quite common in Norway, are rare in Scotland or Ireland. In Scotland, however, the Viking dead are occasionally buried, as they are for example in Denmark, secondarily in prehistoric burial-mounds[95] – a rite not recorded in Man.[96] Graves in single prominent mounds have occasionally been found in England. Two important parallels to the Manx examples are the burials from Hesket-in-the-Forest and Aspatria in Cumbria, almost within sight of the Isle of Man.[97] Both are old finds, the former was discovered in 1822 and the latter in 1789. The mound at Aspatria was 2m high, while the mound at Hesket was described as a cairn and was 6.7m in diameter. Both mounds covered male graves containing a sword, spears and riding equipment. The ornament on the hilt of the Hesket sword is probably to be dated to the early years of the tenth century – the same date as some of the Manx graves.[98]

From the comparatively rich Manx burial material we may begin to understand the early history of Norse settlement in the Island. While there may have been early visits to Man by Scandinavian raiders, it would seem, on the basis of the material found in the mound-graves, that the first Viking settlers arrived in the Island in the final years of the ninth century.[99] Why they had not settled earlier, in view of the obvious strategic importance of the Island in the northern part of the Irish Sea, is difficult to say; but a few suggestions may be considered. In the first place, judging from the poverty of the early Christian culture of the Island, it is unlikely that the Island was wealthy enough

---

93 Wilson 1967, 43-4; See also Edwards, B. J. N. 1992; Halsall 2000, critically re-examined finds of 'Viking' material in English graveyards; his arguments have been followed (briefly) by Hadley 2002, 223-4. His conclusions as to the exiguous evidence of Viking use of churchyards in England are open to question, but in any case need not apply to the much tighter geographical region of Man, where the evidence at Balladoole and St. Patrick's Isle is much more convincing. Richards 2002, 160-5, is less dismissive of the English evidence.

94 O'Brien, 1992; idem., 1998, 217; Ó Floinn, 1998, 145. A more general survey is Harrison 2001.

95 Graham-Campbell and Batey 1998, 29, 145-6 (sometimes in settlement-mounds); secondary burial in mounds is not found in England, Williams, H. 1997, 23. Cf. Pedersen 2006, for Denmark.

96 In 2006 a 'Time Team' excavation for television suggested that the Speke, Braddan, lintel-grave cemetery was centred on a prehistoric – presumably Bronze Age – mound.

97 Edwards, B. J. N. 1992 43-8; other possible mound-burials in this area are old finds from Blackrod (1770) and Billington (1846), ibid., 48. For a modern re-investigation of the Aspatria grave, see Abramson 2000.

98 Wilson 1995a, 48 and fig. 5.

99 Graham-Campbell and I now agree on such a date. Graham-Campbell 1998, 117-8; Wilson 1995/7, 369.

at this period to attract the attention of the initial 'get-rich-quick' raiders, who at best could only expect to get away with a few slaves and provisions, for there was probably little other portable wealth in the Island. Second, in the ninth century, the Vikings had opportunities in Ireland to obtain wealth, both by raiding and trading, which far outstripped anything that could be obtained in the Island. Third, no major beach markets in the Island could challenge those at Whithorn and Luce Sands in Galloway and Meols (on the estuary of the Dee), or the markets at the Viking base of Dublin in Ireland (fig. 4 inset), each of which had rich hinterlands. That there were minor markets in the Isle of Man in the Viking Age is certain, particularly at Ronaldsway (see below p. 117-8); indeed, if there were no such markets early Viking traders would not be tempted to Man. Fourth, as has been mentioned, the tidal system around the Isle of Man is complicated and dangerous; the height of the tide can be more than 10m above low water and currents at certain periods of the tide are extremely strong. Further, much of the coast is unwelcoming, especially in the south-west, where (although there are bays with partly protected beaches) vicious cliffs fall directly into the sea. Consequently, until strangers had learnt to understand the tides and the coast, any approach to the Isle of Man would have been hazardous, especially in bad weather.

The Viking settlement of the Island could have been triggered by various possible factors – either singly or in combination. For example, as those Scandinavians who had settled in the eastern midlands of Ireland in the middle years of the ninth century began to use the Irish Sea more intensively, the strategic potential of the Island would have become more apparent and its control more attainable. Also important was the fact that in the third quarter of the ninth century the Dublin Vikings were active in south-west Scotland, as they brought the whole of southern Pictland under their intermittent control. Further, they broke the power of the Strathclyde Britons in 871 by capturing their fortress at Dumbarton.[100] In so doing they pushed towards Cumbria and the northern part of the Irish Sea. Lastly, towards the end of the ninth century, Danish settlers from the Scandinavian kingdom of York and from Mercia began to settle north-west England and the coast-line of Dumfries and Galloway,[101] which had hitherto been ignored by Irish-Sea Vikings well aware of the difficult sands and lack of safe and easy harbours on that coast. These settlers could have begun to realise that the Isle of Man had economic potential and might be of some strategic importance. Lastly, there was an exodus of Vikings from Dublin, whence many were expelled in 902 to

---

100 Ó Corráin 1998, 330-5.
101 It is noteworthy that only one definite pagan grave is recorded from the south-west of mainland Scotland, adjacent to St. Cuthbert's churchyard, Kirkcudbright. Graham-Campbell 2001, 11-13 and fig. 5.

Fig. 22. Much corroded sword, possibly of Anglo-Saxon manufacture, from a grave in Ballaugh. Surviving length: 31cm.

settle in north-west England, perhaps after a period in Anglesey and the Wirral.[102] The turmoil caused by the presence of Vikings from Dublin in the Scandinavian-controlled north-west of England and south-west Scotland may have encouraged a secondary settlement of Man from this region. They perhaps followed the example of slightly earlier Scandinavian settlers, who may have come to the Island directly from Dublin and the established colonies in the Western Isles – settlers driven by land-hunger in a period when land-taking was endemic in north-west Europe.

102 Ó Corráin 1998, 335-7, has suggested rather that the Vikings of ninth-century Dublin, who had originally come from Scotland, returned after 902 to Scotland and, from there, captured York and re-founded Dublin as a kingdom in 917. This argument has many layers, some more acceptable than others, and, although some of the elements seem correct, it is clear that the expulsion from Dublin put considerable pressure on the Scandinavians of north-west England.

CHAPTER 2

This is a complicated story, but it is against the background of all these events that we must view the Norse settlement of the Isle of Man. The written sources are silent about this land-taking and we must, therefore, rely on the archaeological evidence derived from a study of the grave-goods. It has been shown that there is, among the grave-goods found in the Island, little material definitely produced in Scandinavia. The swords from Knock y Doonee, Cronk Moar and Ballateare are all of Scandinavian type and were almost certainly made in Norway; the same is probably true of one of the spearheads from Ballateare. By contrast most of the other objects (including many weapons) found in the Viking graves are of insular (Irish, English or Scottish) or Continental origin and some, like the hemispherical shield-bosses from Ballateare, Knock y Doonee and Balladoyne, could have been made anywhere in the Viking world.

While the boat-burial rite is Norwegian, the most satisfactory explanation for these mound-burials and the burial at Balladoole is that they represent settlers, who had not come directly from Norway, but from the established settlements in the Scottish islands, or who were displaced refugees from Ireland (who came by way of England). Some may have come directly from the Norse settlements in Ireland, but this is unlikely. Such secondary settlement is probably represented by grave-goods found in pre-existing Christian cemeteries, most clearly seen at St. Patrick's Isle, hardly any of which can definitely have been made in Scandinavia. This is also emphasised by the find of swords of Anglo-Saxon type from Ballabrooie, Maughold and Ballaugh (fig. 22).[103] The burial ritual and the contents of the Manx mound-graves – the real land-takers – reflect those of similar burials in Cumbria, at Aspatria and Hesket-in-the-Forest, whence they perhaps came at the turn of the ninth century. Men of some substance, buried presumably on their newly-won land, they were warriors, advertising by their weapons, their burial-ritual, and, by the prominence of their mounds, their connections with the pagan warlike gods.

Some of the contemporaries of those buried in the mounds were interred in flat graves in existing burial-grounds. Some may have been second-generation settlers. So far no burials with accompanying grave-goods have been found which date later than the 940s. We may, therefore, safely assume that by the middle of the tenth century the Viking incomers had settled down and become Christian, a date supported by the date of sculptured memorials discussed below.

The native inhabitants must have been overwhelmed by the initial force of the land-taking; but they would have had to be mollified in some manner, otherwise the incomers would have been unable to sleep at night. The numbers of incoming Vikings would not have been large (Basil Megaw hazarded a guess at a force of some 400), but they would have been tough, frightening and predatory. As is shown in the next chapter, the two elements of the population on occasion intermarried; thus a *modus vivendi*

---

103 Wilson 2008. The swords are of Petersen 1919, type L.

must to a certain extent have been achieved, based on brute force on the part of the incomers, on the threat of outside allies on the part of the locals, or on bribery – or on a combination of all three. The fact that the incomers were pagan in a Christian environment must have set up tensions. Perhaps, indeed, Christianity was the agent that ultimately helped to solve the tensions between the two communities – a tension which was apparently released fairly quickly.

The absence of later pagan burials and the survival of a large group of tenth-century carved stone crosses, mostly found in or around the keeills or in what are now parish churchyards, demonstrate that the Scandinavian incomers to the Island quickly converted to Christianity – probably within a generation. What this meant in terms of religious experience, political expediency or sincerity cannot be resolved. The 'pagan' Scandinavians had no organised equivalent of the Christian Church and, although we have some perception of their mythology (some represented in the Island, below p. 82-4), which is clearly related to figures defined as 'gods', there is no clear evidence of the depth of religious thought and experience behind it – other than the presence of a pagan burial rite. The rite of unaccompanied burial in a Christian manner occurs both before and after the Scandinavian incursions, and there is no evidence of native accompanied burial for many centuries before the Viking Age.

The carved stone monuments considered in the next chapter are crucial to an understanding of the development of Scandinavian settlement in the Island. Taken together, the graves and memorials provide a framework for the history of the settlement and of the cultural identity of the society in Man in the tenth century.

From paganism to Christianity

The memorial crosses and their ornament

The process of the conversion of the Manx Vikings to Christianity is difficult to trace. Nothing is known of their formal relations with the Church, save what can be gleaned from archaeological evidence. Changing burial rites – the gradual end of accompanied burial – demonstrate that at some time in the first quarter of the tenth century the new religion began to take hold. Further, the presence of a large body of memorial sculpture in the Isle of Man, because of its concentration in a limited geographic area, provides an unique insight into the process of conversion to Christianity of a pagan Viking population. With its English counterparts, Manx memorial sculpture provides the earliest physical evidence of conversion to Christianity in the Scandinavian world. What is more, the ornament of the sculpture not only provides important and close links with mainstream Scandinavian art, but also demonstrates, through its iconography, an important perception of the interface between paganism and Christianity.

A great deal is known, through oral memory preserved in twelfth- and thirteenth-century literature, of the pagan gods of Scandinavia, of their attributes and of the myths which surrounded them; but little is known of pagan religious practices.[1] Although there is an eleventh-century German description of a major temple and of religious rites based on idols of the pagan gods at Uppsala in Sweden, physical evidence concerning it is non-existent, and the description – while probably true – is flimsy and exaggerated.[2] There is certainly no physical evidence of temples, idols or pagan rites (other than burial practices) anywhere in the British Isles in the Viking Age. There are, however, occasional hints of the existence of the pagan incomers' religion in the place-names (even in the Isle of Man, see p. 102).

Written Icelandic sources seem to show that strong secular men (local chiefs – *goði* – of the highest rank) largely organised the pagan religion as cult-priests who carried out its rituals in their houses or in the open air. Whether there were such pagan characters and practices in the Isle of Man is unknown, and, as elsewhere in the Viking world, we know nothing about the strength of their beliefs. What is clear is that the Scandinavian settlers in Man and their descendants – as elsewhere in the British Isles – soon became

---

1 An excellent (English) summary of the literary evidence for Scandinavian paganism is Sørensen 1997.
2 Olsen 1966, 116-66.

Christian. We do not know how this affected their lives or behaviour; we only know that, as they converted, their burial rite changed. Mound-burial had ceased to be practised at an early stage of the settlement and, as we have seen on St. Patrick's Isle, the rite of accompanied burial petered out, probably early in the second quarter of the tenth century.

Stone memorials

Although the Scandinavians of the early Viking Age apparently often raised a wooden post on top of a mound (as at Ballateare, p. 32), there were no stone memorials in their homeland. Even ornamented stone sculpture was unknown before the Viking Age, with the exception of carving on monuments on the far-away Swedish island of Gotland (a type of historiated carving which is, in style and content, almost completely unrelated to that of the rest of Western Europe[3]). When the pagan incomers to the Island began to bury their dead in existing cemeteries they presumably became familiar with the earlier stone grave-markers and, as they converted to Christianity, quickly adopted the native form of memorial for their own dead, as Viking settlers did enthusiastically in England and, to a lesser degree, in western and northern Scotland, where standing stones featuring the Christian cross were also erected.[4] In Man they carved their stone memorial slabs from local soft grey slate or mudstone.[5] Ornamented on one or both sides, and occasionally on the edges, the stones were presumably grave-markers, or at least memorials to the dead.[6] The cross remained the chief feature on the Manx stones, and the word 'cross' (*krus*) appears in many of the inscriptions as a descriptor of the memorial itself, presumably also emphasising a religion new to the Viking settlers and their families. Some elements of the form of the cross-heads were adapted by the Viking

---

3 Lindqvist 1941.

4 One specific form of Viking memorial, the recumbent hog-backed tombstone, popular in northern England and southern Scotland (Lang 1984), does not occur in the Island. Bailey 1985, 55, suggests that their absence is due to the fact that Manx slate was ill-suited to the production of such monuments.

5 It is sometimes stated that two stones from Kirk Braddan are of imported sandstone; geological examination (D. Quirk, personal communication) confirms that they all belong to the Manx Series.

6 The crosses are identified by numbers affixed to the stones, the primary inventory number given by Manx National Heritage. The number in brackets refers (where applicable) to the standard corpus, Kermode 1994 (originally published in 1907; the second edition is used here as it contains a new introduction, a bibliography from 1907-95, and a reprint of Kermode's supplementary articles on new finds up to 1929). A number of attempts have been made to re-number the stones, most recently – and perhaps most logically – in an unpublished Ph.D thesis: Trench-Jellicoe 1985. His numeration is now used by a number of scholars, particularly epigraphers, but in view of the lack of easy access to the thesis I have retained the old system of numeration and used it here.

settlers from native Manx models.[7] The ornament of the carving is consistent with the incomers' stylistic taste, which had its roots in Scandinavia. Further, many crosses bear inscriptions incised in runic characters which, with two exceptions, memorialise the dead. These are written in the settlers' own language (Old West Norse) in a script of Norwegian form.[8] Most of these stones have been found casually over the centuries, none has been found in association with a burial and none has been scientifically excavated. Most, if not all of them, were found in cemeteries which had been in use before the Vikings came to the Island. It is even conceivable that some stones were erected over furnished burials like those discussed in the previous chapter.

A few stones stood in the open air for many hundreds of years (although most have now been brought indoors); many more were discovered in the nineteenth and twentieth centuries, built into walls or buried in the ground. Most are fragmentary and many have eroded surfaces. Now presenting a sombre appearance, they were probably originally enlivened by colour. There is growing evidence that Viking memorial sculpture in both Scandinavia and England was emphasised by the use of paint, usually red and black, but occasionally white, although surviving occurrences are rare and usually only noticed on newly-found pieces.[9] No traces of colour have been found on stones in the Manx corpus, but it is quite possible that colour was originally used to enhance the carved patterns and even to add detail and inscriptions to them (even on those stones with the finest carvings). In general, the Viking-age stones demonstrate a good deal of skill on the part of the sculptors. Some are more muddled or more complicated in their image than others, whilst a few are of extremely high quality, particularly two of the Braddan stones, 135 (108) and 136 (109) (figs. 28 and 29), and one of those from Andreas, 128 (102). Some seem to be carved incompetently, as, for example, the misnamed Roolwer stone from Maughold, 98 (72) (fig. 34). Most stones are dated to the tenth century, by reference to their ornament, which may be set against an accepted Scandinavian chronology. Those stones which have little ornament, or ornament less clearly related to a particular art style, can be dated by reference to the form of the cross or by comparison with details elsewhere. Thus, for example Lonan 73 (57) (fig. 23), which has no animal ornament, may be dated by its general ornamental relationship to the form and interlace treatment of a cross from Kirk Braddan 72 (69),[10] which has animal-ornamented panels of which one (fig. 24, top left) is unquestionably of Scandinavian form. Interestingly, these two cross-heads have exactly the same diameter, which might imply that they were made by the same craftsman.

---

7 This is seen if one compares the form of the cross on stone from Ballavarkish, Bride, 52, Kermode 1994, fig. B. 15, which has eighth-century graffiti, with the Lonan cross 73 (57) (fig. 23), which belongs to the Viking Age.
8 Page 1983.
9 Jansson 1987, 153-60. The English evidence has been summarised by Bailey 1996a, 32-4.
10 Kermode 1994, pl. 27.

Fig. 23. Lonan 78 (57). Diam. of head: 96cm. *Fig. 24. Braddan 72 (69). Diam. of head: 96cm.*

The exact number of surviving sculptures of Viking-age date in the Island is hard to estimate, but a figure of about seventy is usually quoted, of which rather less than half have inscriptions. This is clearly an underestimate as many stones once thought to have belonged to the period before the Vikings came to the Island are now generally accepted as of Viking-age date (see chapter 1), and the total must be nearer a hundred.[11] The tallest complete example of a stone of the Viking Age is nearly 4m in height (Rushen 100 (76)) – the ornament of which has now completely disappeared) – and the smallest measures less than a metre. Many carved stones, however, survive only as fragments. All but one – in Lonan parish churchyard, 73 (57) (fig. 23) – have been moved from their original position, and we cannot even be certain that the Lonan cross was never shifted. As at Lonan, many seem to have been set in sockets cut out of flatish stones large enough to give them stability. In some cases a tenon was cut at the base of a slab, which fitted into a socket, as on the cross from Ballaugh, 106 (77) (fig. 25). Kermode records that the cross from Braddan 135 (108) (fig. 28), 'has a tongue-shaped prolongation for

---

11 This re-identification has been made possible by the critical approach of Trench-Jellicoe 1988.

insertion through a socket into the ground', which measured 68cm.[12] Memorial stones of Scandinavian type occur in every Island parish except Arbory.

The ornament on many of the Viking-age stones is basically Scandinavian, although there are elements of contemporary north English and even Scottish and Irish taste. Much of the ornament is purely decorative; space is filled with interlaced ribbons and the ribbons themselves are sometimes embellished with double contours and billets. In a long tradition common to northern European art of the post-Roman period, some of this ornamental space-filling takes the form of contorted animals, the bodies of which interlace with their own limbs and sometimes with other animals or ribbons. The meaning of many such motifs has been long forgotten and may not even have been understood by the sculptor himself. Other motifs on the stones clearly have symbolic significance, either in Christian terms or in Norse mythological tradition. Some single animals are clearly recognisable – deer, for example – and some of them combine into scenes which are familiar iconographic constructs elsewhere. The 'hart and hound' motif seen on some stones is known from Roman times, but also occurs in Pictish/Scottish sculpture of an entirely different iconographical

Fig. 25. Ballaugh 106 (77). Photograph, c. 1890, showing the tenon which would have slotted into a stone base. Height: 1.37m.

tradition. The riders depicted on some stones are possibly, as was stated in the previous chapter, representative of the journey of a warrior to the after-life, to the pagan Valhalla. Iconographical interpretation of the motifs on the Manx crosses has been a feature of scholarship over many years. In the early years of their study scholars, particularly Philip Kermode, were sometimes over-optimistic in their pioneering identification of the scenes on the stones. Nowadays we are more cautious – more sceptical – and

12 Kermode 1994, 203.

*Fig. 26. Michael
101 (74). Memorial
stone carved by
Gautr. Height:
1.8m.*

E.W.

this cautious scepticism is reflected here. The style of the ornament on the crosses, however, is important in another context in that it enables us to put most of the stones into a coherent series, dating from about 925 to 1000. As this is of some consequence in building up the sequence of Norse settlement of the Island, it is worth considering its chronology before discussing the pictorial content of the sculpture itself.

Four Scandinavian art styles are present in the Isle of Man; all are named after sites in Scandinavia.[13] The Borre style, the dominant style in Man, of which the feature most relevant to the Manx series is the ring-chain ornament on the stem of the cross from Kirk Michael 101 (74) (fig. 26) is in Scandinavia dated to the period *c.* 890-960. The Jellinge style, which is best seen on the stem of the cross from Malew 94 (120) (fig. 27), is rare in the Island. Its chief feature is a ribbon-like animal with a double contour. It

---

13 Recently summarised by Wilson 1995, 87-115. For a discussion of the styles in English see Wilson and Klindt-Jensen 1966.

CHAPTER 3

Fig. 27. Malew 120 (94). The animal in the shaft of the cross, left, is of classic Jellinge style. Scenes from the Sigurd legend can be seen on the panel far right: at the top Sigurd has burnt his finger: below he can just be made out killing the dragon. The story is made more easily comprehensible if compared with fig. 40. Height: 1.5m.

 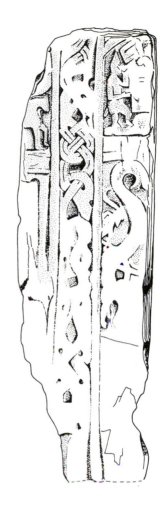

is dated *c.*910-60. The Mammen style is best seen on Braddan 135 (108) and 136 (109) (figs. 28 and 29). Their animals have substantial billeted bodies with fleshy leaf-like extensions. They date from the middle years of the tenth century. Towards the end of the tenth century the Ringerike style replaces the Mammen and Jellinge styles (which are partly contemporary). Only one or two elements of this style can be traced on the Manx crosses – the eye on Kirk Michael 117 (89) (fig. 30), for example.

Kirk Michael, 101 (74) (fig. 26) is usually assumed – rightly or wrongly[14] – to be one of the earliest complete crosses. On one edge (and running over onto the top of one face) is a runic inscription which reads in translation: 'Mailbrikti, son of Aþakán, smith, raised this cross for his soul … Gautr made this and all in Man'.[15] On one face

---

14 Cf. Page, 1983, 136-8.
15 For a transcription and normalisation of the original text of this and all the Manx Viking-age inscriptions see Page 1983, 140-1.

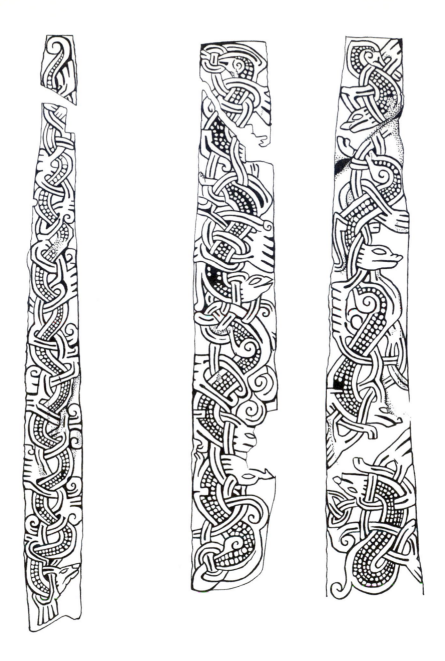

Fig. 28. Ornament of memorial cross, Braddan 135 (108). Length of field shown: 1.45m.

E.W.

Fig. 29. Ornament of memorial cross, Braddan 136 (109). Length: 1.22m.

is a ring-headed cross, the stem of which is ornamented with a Borre-style 'ring-chain' interlace pattern. The three arms at the head of the cross are ornamented with a – slightly clumsy – developed version of this motif. The shaft of the cross on the other face and the panels below the arms on both faces are decorated with various interlace patterns of types which are also found either in Scandinavia or in Viking contexts in England. On one of the lateral panels is an asymmetrical tendril pattern, basically a coarse version of the classic English version of the vine-scroll. Some interlace panels on this stone, particularly those with foliate terminations, are from a developed stage of the style and indicate a date in the second quarter of the tenth century. In the inscription Gautr boasts that he 'made this and all in Man'. It is possible that Gautr may only have carved the stone and not the inscription, for there is an inscription on another slab (Andreas 99 (73)), which causes the runologist Raymond Page – on the evidence of the runes only – to remark, 'the texts look to be by different rune-carvers', acknowledging, however, that this is a subjective judgement.[16] It is possible that, as is documented on Swedish rune-stones, the rune-master and the carver of the ornament were two separate people.[17] Indeed, this is likely in this case, for, while the style of the inscription is different, the execution of the ornament on the two stones bearing Gautr's name is very similar. On these stones the uniting element is a simple Borre ring-chain motif, which also occurs on a number of other memorials.

While not every stone decorated with the true Borre ring-chain can definitely be attributed to the sculptor Gautr, some can be ascribed to him on stylistic grounds.[18] The fragmentary stone from Nappin, Jurby 103 (78), provides a convincing parallel (although the ring-chain here occurs on one of the side panels and not on the stem of the cross), as it also bears a motif similar to the foliate motif on Gautr's Kirk Michael stone. Other stones, with a more elaborate version of the Borre ring-chain, are almost certainly by other, later, hands. Such, for example, is Ballaugh 106 (77) (fig. 25), where the ribbons of the interlace on the stem of the cross (as distinct from those in one of the side panels) are billeted in a similar manner to the interlace on that from Braddan (fig. 135) which is decorated in the rather later Mammen style.

An interesting development of the Borre-style interlace occurs in the ornamental treatment of the cross-head, which takes a number of rather elaborate – often awkward – forms, seen in one of its most competent manifestations on Gautr's cross at Kirk Michael. Interestingly; it also occurs on crosses which have no other specific Borre-style features in their interlace. Indeed, on some of the latest ornamented stones – Kirk Michael 117 (89), for example – the memory of the Borre style lingers on the head of the cross, while animal ornament elsewhere on the slab is generally of a later date and different style. Similar motifs are found on English cross-heads; indeed, Richard Bailey derives the English versions of this treatment from the Island.[19] He has also proposed that the tendril motif found on one side of Gautr's cross and on a number of other Manx slabs, which occurs on sculptured stones in northern England, was also derived from the Island and ultimately from Scandinavia. Leaf ornament, however, is rare in Scandinavia until the middle of the tenth century. It is more likely that this particular motif, although developed in the Island, was based on contemporary English sources, where ornament derived, as is this, from the vine-scroll is commonly found,[20] and that it was exported from Man to the North of England.

---

16 Page 1983, 136.
17 Wilson and Klindt-Jensen 1966, 151-2.
18 For example, Michael 102 (75), St. John's 107 (81) and Braddan 112 (86). If one extends this list to include ring-chains with a double ribbon, one might add stones like Maughold 108 (82) and (more doubtfully because of the associated ornament) Bride 118 (92).
19 Bailey 1980, 219-20.
20 E.g. Wilson 1984, figs. 192 and 203.

Fig. 30. Detail of Michael 117 (89). Note the form of the eye, one of the diagnostic features of the Ringerike style.

In more general terms, the Manx stones decorated in the Borre style – of which, as has been shown, there are a fair number – tend to belong to a late period of the style's development (between say 925 and 960). On the Ballaugh stone, it gradually edges into a more florid treatment which presages (and even overlaps with) the arrival of the next two (partly contemporaneous) styles – Jellinge and Mammen. The interlace at the top of Andreas 131 (103) (fig. 31), for example, has moved away from the carefully balanced forms encountered on the Gautr group of crosses to an asymmetrical, free-flowing, lush knot which is close to knots on objects decorated in the Scandinavian Mammen style.[21] Pure Jellinge-style elements are rare on Manx crosses. Classically, however, the style is seen in the ribbon-like, double-contoured animal on the stem of a cross from Malew (fig. 27), which is closely related to the ornament on the small silver cup from the royal burial at Jelling, Denmark, which gave the style its name.[22]

The Mammen style is seen at its best on two crosses from Kirk Braddan (figs. 28 and 29), where it is as accomplished and as pure as any found in its Viking homelands.[23] So untainted is it by any Anglo-Saxon or British overtones, and so true is it to the form of the style as it appears in Scandinavia, that it has even been suggested, on chronological grounds, that the style was developed in the Island, or at least in the

---

21 Cf. e.g., the asymmetrical floriated interlace on the Mammen axe itself, Wilson 1995, fig. 107.
22 Ibid., figs. 95 and 96.
23 Fuglesang 1991.

Fig. 31. Andreas 131 (103). One of the largest of the Manx stones, portraying a possible hunting scene. Height: 1.9m.

Fig. 32. The Heðinn stone, Maughold 142. To the right is the lightly incised image of a ship with furled sail. Surviving height: 76cm.

Fig. 33. Onchan 141 (113). Memorial stone with cross and runic inscription, set up by a man in memory of his wife who had a Celtic name, Murkialu. Height: 143cm.

Irish Sea region.[24] While this is unlikely, there are few better examples of the classic Mammen style than those found in the Isle of Man. Basically the artist who developed this style plumped out the body of the ribbon-like Jellinge-style animal and filled it with billets (a typical feature). The spiral hips became more pronounced; lush foliate elements were introduced into the interlace, and the snout became more rounded.

---

24 For a summary of the arguments see Graham-Campbell 1995, 41-7.

Fig. 34. Maughold 98 (72). The so-called 'Roolwer Stone'. Kermode unsuccessfully attempted to associate it with 'Hrólfr', an eleventh-century bishop. The ornament is very muddled, but a botched attempt to carve a hunting scene appears on either side of the lower half of the cross-shaft. Height: approx. 92cm.

Mammen-style animals are also present at the base of a cross on one of the faces of a stone from Kirk Michael, 132 (105), and elements of the style of less pure form may be seen in the ornament of one or two other pieces.[25] Interestingly, it has been proposed, on the basis of the Mammen style ornament engraved on them, that four of the great silver brooches in the Skaill hoard in Orkney, which was probably deposited after 950, were made in Man.[26] The ornament on these brooches is remarkably similar to that found on the Braddan crosses, and there is no inherent reason why this should not be so. While tenth-century metalwork with animal ornament of this quality has not been found in the Island, and, while there is no evidence of its production here, the quality of the craftsmanship of the Manx Mammen ornament makes this at least a possibility. (In the early eleventh century one of the gold rings from the Greeba hoard – pp 114-5 – was probably made in the Island and shows that fine metalwork could have been produced here a few years later.)

25 Kermode 1994, pl. lv, 105a. See also pl. li.
26 Graham-Campbell 1995, 72, 42-3.

Fig. 35. Surviving fragment of a crucifixion plaque from the Calf of Man, Rushen, 61 (50). Height: 66cm.

The ornament of the Greeba ring (fig. 54) belongs to the Ringerike style, which is only minimally present in the Manx sculptural corpus. The eyes of the animals in the side panels of Kirk Michael 117 (89) (fig. 30) have heads with a single typically Ringerike element – a pear-shaped eye with its point towards the snout. Its presence, however slight, indicates the end of Scandinavian ornamental styles on the Manx stones.

This Kirk Michael stone also represents the apparent end, *c.* 1000, of the custom of erecting stones in memory of the dead. Indeed, there is only one decorated stone which is probably of later date, Maughold 142 (fig. 32), and this retains only a pale reflection of the richly ornamented Manx crosses.[27] It bears an inscription on the face of the stone, recording that it was raised by a man called Heðinn in memory of his daughter, and that a man called Arni cut the runes. As distinct from the normal Norwegian of the Manx runes, some of the vocabulary and runes on this stone show Danish influence (although there is clearly still a Norwegian input). The form of the letter **e** encountered in this inscription seems to have entered Danish runic epigraphy about 1000 (in Norway it was introduced rather later), thus it is possible to date this stone after the main body of the Manx series, at some time in the early eleventh century.[28] The Danish runes may reflect the growing power of Denmark in England at the beginning of the eleventh century, a continuation of the cross-fertilisation of ideas and influences between England and Man which had started long before the Viking Age. The presence of an incised ship of 'Viking type' on

27 Kermode 1994, fig. C9.
28 Page 1983, 137.

the cross may be of no recoverable significance (it may indeed be an added graffito), but it is worth noting that the earliest heraldic device of the Kingdom of Man and the Isles – first recorded in the twelfth century – was just such a ship.[29]

If the Heðinn stone is apparently the last of the Scandinavian series, what came afterwards? The plain, often linear, crosses which apparently formed the headstones of Christian graves have been mentioned above (p. 58). There is absolutely no dating evidence for these monuments, even when they have been properly excavated, as for example at Keeill Vael in Druidale and on St. Patrick's Isle.[30] Such stones are paralleled in Wales, Scotland and Ireland and may as easily date from after the Viking period as before. Further, among the stones which bear more elaborately delineated wheel-head crosses but which are otherwise undecorated, there are almost certainly some which are of Viking-age date; others may belong to a period after the main Scandinavian Manx series ends.[31] One of the plain wheel-head crosses from Onchan 141 (113) (fig. 33) has a long inscription in Norse runes which indicates that some of the plain incised crosses of similar form may well be of tenth-century date.[32]

Much work remains to be done on the crosses which are decorated with interlace patterns and motifs not easily related either to the recognisably Viking ornamental styles, or to other styles of the countries around the Irish Sea. One stone, for example, the so-called Roolwer stone, Maughold 98 (72) (fig. 34), is so clumsy and incompetent in the execution of its eclectic motifs that it is impossible to date it or to place it in a stylistic sequence, although the form of the interlace would include it within the Viking series.[33]

A fragmentary carved slab, perhaps an altar-frontal rather than a memorial stone, from the Calf of Man, 61 (50) (fig. 35), was for many years thought to be pre-Viking, but, following a perspicacious lecture by the late Basil Megaw (which was never published), it is now generally accepted that it is of late Viking-age date.[34] The slab bears a Crucifixion scene. Christ, nailed to the cross, has a forked beard and long hair, which, parted in the middle, forms a spiral curl on his shoulder. There is an omega-like motif on his forehead. His robes are formalised; in the centre of his chest is a roundel of double-strand ribbon interlace, his sleeves and cloak are panelled and a four-looped interlace appears below the central roundel. Above the hem of his tunic are a pelta-like double spiral figure and a continuous ribbon formed of three pointed loops, known as a triquetra. The right-hand side of the panel is missing, but to the left, below the cross arm, is the figure of the spear-bearer, Longinus, a bearded figure with long flowing hair. The scene was originally compared with that on a bronze openwork plaque said to be from St John's,

29 Megaw 1959-60; Goodall 2004.
30 Trench-Jellicoe in Morris 1983, 126-8; Trench-Jellicoe 2002.
31 E.g. Kermode 1994, pls. xi, 31 and xii, 35 and 38.
32 Ibid., pl. lxi and, for a comparator, pl. xi, 31.
33 Ibid., pl. xxviii.
34 Wilson 2008, for all references.

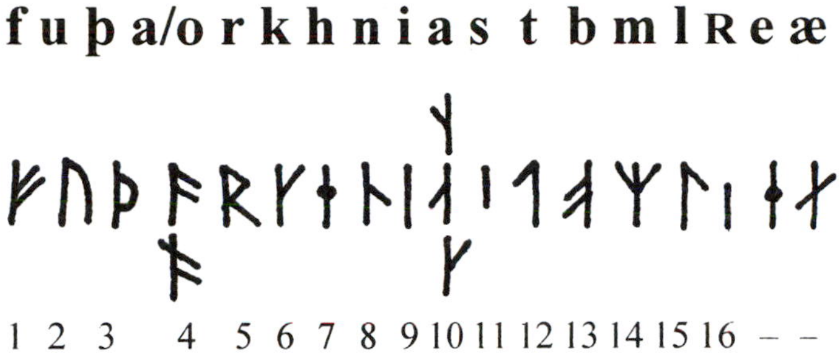

f u þ a/o r k h n i a s t b m l R e æ

1 2 3   4 5 6 7 8 9 10 11 12 13 14 15 16 – –

Fig. 36. The Manx fuþark (alphabet). The third character has the value 'th'. The characters (including variations from the norm) are numbered according to their order in the 16-character (short-twig) fuþark which was introduced into Man in the tenth century (alternate forms of nos. 4 and 10 are shown). Two other runic letters have been introduced for ease of reference: e occurs on two stones (there is no h – which has a similar form – in either inscription), while æ occurs only once. Runes of Danish type which occur on Kirk Michael 130 (104) are somewhat different in form (see Page 1983, 141). On the late stone, Maughold 142 (fig. 32), the runes are modified and classified as 'mixed' (Page, loc.cit.). Andreas 111 (84) has cryptic runes, which cannot be interpreted. Forms may differ in non-significant ways (e.g. curved rather than straight lines) from those shown here.

Rinnagan, near Athlone, Co. Roscommon.[35] Although both Christ and Longinus on this plaque are unbearded and lack the flowing hair, there is an undoubted general concurrence between the two designs. Further, although Christ's tunic is less elaborately panelled, the wings of the angels on the plaque reflect the hatching on the Calf tunic. The Athlone plaque, however, differs in both style and detail from the Calf panel, and the best parallels are with a group of similar bronze plaques, all from Ireland, and all save one executed in openwork, clearly made to be placed on a wooden base – on a shrine or book-cover perhaps. Their dating is controversial, although a pre-Viking-age date is generally agreed;[36] but one plaque, from Clonmacnoise, is very different.[37] The foliate ornament, on this plaque is clearly an element from the Irish version of the Ringerike style, thus a late tenth- or early eleventh-century date for it seems reasonably robust. The Calf of Man crucifixion scene is closely related to the Clonmacnoise plaque. The spirals on the wings of the angels on the plaque compare well with those on the stone, and on both pieces Christ is bearded and the supporting figures are in profile.

Outside Ireland the most interesting sculptural parallel to the Calf Crucifixion scene – and one recently much discussed – is a painted stone panel from Penrith which,

---

35 Harbison 1984.
36 But see Bourke 1993.
37 Ibid., fig. 21.1a.

Fig. 37. Memorial stone, Michael 129 (101). Left: the manner in which runic inscriptions are normally positioned. The fragmentary inscription reads from the bottom: (k) r i m s: i n s: s u a r t a. The first word is presumably a personal name (possibly Grim), a man with the nickname 'the Black'. The 'x' signifies the end of the inscription. Surviving height of stone: 47cm. Right: Crucifixion in middle of cross-head.

though cruder in composition, has features common to both the Calf stone and the Clonmacnoise mount. As on the Clonmacnoise mount the bearded figure of Christ is fully clothed, unlike that on most other contemporary stones. The Penrith panel has been tentatively dated to the tenth century.[38] Crucifixion scenes occur in Hiberno-Saxon manuscripts from the late seventh or early eighth century onwards, but a scene more clearly related to that on the Calf stone occurs in the early eleventh-century Irish Southampton Psalter (St John's College, Cambridge, MS C9)[39], where the formalised clothes and beard of Christ are in some sort of sequence with the Calf stone and the Clonmacnoise plaque, although (presumably because of the different media) subject to rather different treatment.

38 Bailey and Cramp 1988, 140-2.
39 Henry 1967, pl. 45.

Runic inscriptions

The decorated stones of the Viking Age reflect a wealthy stratum of society. Only more substantial families could afford to raise such elaborate memorials over their dead, memorials which must in some ways be equivalent to the rich mound-burials of the pagan settlers discussed in the previous chapter. They tell us much about the people commemorated. First, the ornament on the stones demonstrates that there were artists and patrons in the Island in sympathy with the decorative repertoire of tenth-century Norway. To a large extent (but not entirely) they eschewed Anglo-Saxon taste, and were, as will be shown, also influenced to a minor degree by the art of western Scotland. The artists were, however, independently minded enough to adapt the Scandinavian ornament to a new medium, stone, which they did not use in their homelands. That they were in close touch with Scandinavia is demonstrated not only by the ornament they used, but also by their use of the Norse runic alphabet (fig. 36),[40] itself indicative of the upper levels of an hierarchical society. The use of runes is unusual in the western seaways of Viking Britain; only one runic-inscribed memorial stone is known from Ireland and three from the Western Isles of Scotland (of which one, from Iona, is a recumbent slab). Twenty-nine inscribed stones have been found in the Northern Isles (excluding the vast, idiosyncratic and puzzling twelfth-century Maeshowe inscriptions[41]), while there are more than thirty inscriptions (some very fragmentary) from Man, as against some forty from Norway. The Manx inscriptions, therefore – however formulaic – considerably enhance knowledge of the Viking Age in the west.

The inscriptions are normally formed by v-shaped cuts on the edge of the stone (fig. 37). In one case (Michael 101 (74) (fig. 26) they spill over from the edge onto the main face, and in a few cases, as Ballaugh 106 (77) (fig. 25) and Onchan 141 (113) (fig. 33), for example, they are carved on the main face itself. The edge of the stone is a logical place for such an inscription as it forms a convenient frame for the main elements of the runic characters, which are usually cut in a straight line. Placing inscriptions on the edge of the stone is unusual in the Scandinavian world, particularly on ornamented stones. Some are to be found on the undecorated stones in the Northern Isles;[42] but elsewhere in the British Isles edge inscriptions are rare, the most striking exception being the early eleventh-century stone from St Paul's churchyard in London.[43] In Norway, an edge inscription occurs most famously on the Alstad stone, which is contemporary

---

40 It must be emphasized that, as well as a number of early stones inscribed in the Latin and ogham scripts, there are two inscriptions in Anglo-Saxon runes in the Island, although they are almost certainly earlier in date than the Norse settlements, Page 1999, 138-9, 143-5. The Island, a Christian entity, was naturally familiar with epigraphic inscriptions before the coming of the Vikings.

41 Barnes 1994.

42 Barnes and Page 2006, 119-214.

43 Wilson 1974a.

Fig. 38. Maughold 145 (115). Stone with inscriptions in runic and ogham characters. The runic inscription reads, i u a n + b r i s t + r a i s t i + þ a s i r + r u n u r + [f] u þ a r k h n i a s t b m l (Juan priest raised these runes – followed by the runic alphabet). Below is the first half of the ogham alphabet: B L F S N H D T C Q. Length of stone: 33cm.

with that from London (although the inscription runs over onto the main ornamented face).[44] In Denmark, where the inscriptions largely occur on granite blocks which do not easily split into thin slabs, inscriptions usually appear on the face of the memorial; while Swedish inscriptions (of which there are some 3,500) are displayed in a very different fashion and edge-inscriptions are rare.[45]

The inscriptions record not only the names of the dead and those who raised stones to their memory ('X raised this cross in memory of Y'), they also tell of sculptors like Gautr, whom we have encountered at Kirk Michael and Andreas, and Arni on Maughold 142 (fig. 32), who 'cut the runes'. We are also (uniquely) told that Gautr, who on one cross is given a patronymic (son of Bjarnar), came from *Kuli* – a place with a Celtic name which is difficult to identify, but is clearly somewhere in western Britain. The names

---

44 Jacobsen 1933, pl. III and IV.
45 But see the stone from Rute, Gotland, where the main inscription is continued on the edge, Jansson 1987, 59.

CHAPTER 3

on the crosses tell their own stories.[46] Most are raised by men in memory of men, but no cross raised by a woman is known (although this happens occasionally in Sweden). At least seven women are commemorated by name in the inscriptions[47] – apparently anonymously in the case of Maughold 142, but usually recorded, as on Andreas 131 (103). In this case the cross (fig. 31) was raised by a man called Sandulf the Black (*santulf hin suarti*) in memory of his wife, Arinbjorg (*arinbiaurk*). Intermarriage between the two communities is clearly suggested – if not directly indicated – in a number of inscriptions. On Kirk Michael 130 (104) a man, Malymkun, put up a memorial to his foster-daughter, a woman with a Gaelic name (Malmury), who was the daughter of a man with a Gaelic name, Dufgal (*tufkal*), yet was married to a man with a Norse name – Aþisl – which seems the likeliest interpretation of a most confusing inscription. The inscription on Braddan 135 (108), mentions a son with a Norse name whose father had a Gaelic name. If these names are those of people of Manx origin and not camp-followers or foreign wives, it would indicate that there were few social barriers between the two communities.

On Gautr's cross, the smith, Aþakan (equivalent of Irish *Aedhacán*), and his son, Melbrigti (*Máelbrigte*) both have Gaelic names. This is significant in that this stone is always considered to be one of the earliest Viking-age crosses on the Island; further, a man with a Norse name carved it. The stone may not then be indicative – as are most of the stones – of conversion to the new religion, as these two native Manxmen were presumably Christian before the incomers arrived, or at least came from a Christian family. This again witnesses to the toleration of Christianity by the incomers. Apart from the rune-writer and the sculptor mentioned above, the only trade recorded is that of the smith on Gautr's cross. Smiths had an important position in the social hierarchy and were presumably wealthy, as is demonstrated by the fact that some of the richest pagan graves in Norway were those of smiths, who were buried with the tools of their trade. The reason for their status is not far to seek, for smiths were the suppliers of weapons, on the reliability of which a man's life could often depend. One legendary smith in particular, Vǫlundr, is known widely in northern European literature; in English his name is usually rendered as Weland or Weyland. The tools of the treacherous smith Regin are almost certainly represented on a stone from Ramsey (122 (96)) (fig. 41).[48]

There is a surprising dearth of Christian formulae in the inscriptions, despite the fact that they appear on stones decorated with the prime Christian symbol, the cross. The main exception being that the Manx inscriptions (plus one in Ireland and one in Bute) refer to the raising of a cross (using the word **krus**); whereas in the few cases in Scandinavia where inscribed memorial crosses are found the normal word used is 'stone'

---

46 The names are listed and analysed by Olsen 1954, 228-32.
47 Maughold 142 and 175, Kirk Michael 130 (44) and 132 (105), Andreas 131 (103) and German 140 (112).
48 Margeson 1983, 101.

(**steinn**).[49] One of the few Christian sentiments occurs on Gautr's stone, 101 (74) (fig. 26), which relates that the cross was raised 'for his soul'. Other Christian references occur in two runic inscriptions from the parish of Maughold – 144 (114) and 145 (115) (fig. 38). These are later than the main series – probably of late twelfth-century date – and are difficult to place in context, as the scripts are archaising; they are unornamented and record the name of a priest called John (*iuan brist*) who apparently lived in Cornaa (*i kurnaþal*); no. 144 also refers to Christ and to three Irish saints. The two stones may well have been carved by a man with antiquarian leanings, proud of his knowledge of runes (and, in the case of 145, of ogham).[50] Another similarly puzzling – but presumably secondary – inscription on a stone of the main Viking-age series, Kirk Michael 130 (104), consists of two lines of ogham, one of which is an alphabet. When these were carved is a mystery, presumably they were executed by a post-Viking-age hand.[51]

Runes were not, contrary to popular belief, generally either secret or magical (although there are cryptic examples – as Andreas 111), but were meant to be read by the (presumably not very numerous) literate. In the twelfth century, for example, wooden tallies or labels discarded in the harbour area at Bergen, Norway, record the ownership of goods and must, therefore, have been written in a script familiar to a merchant's clerk.[52] A more unusual Manx cross-slab – unusual in that it bears no elaborate ornament and has inscriptions which may have been carved by more than one hand – comes from Onchan 141 (113) (fig. 33). The text, which is unique, reads in translation, 'I think about [the runes] and interpret [? read] them properly'. Its meaning has baffled runologists for years, and runologists are rarely baffled.

Although the Manx stones, belong to the same period as the earliest inscribed Scandinavian stones, they are textually different. A number of Scandinavian stones, while memorialising a dead person, have a semi-legal status, celebrating the completion of a work of public benefit – such as building a bridge, marking roads, or recording land-holding. Such textual formulae are not found in Man.

Iconography of the stones

A fascinating aspect of Manx Viking sculpture is the presence of a large number of individual animal and human figures, most of which presumably have iconographic significance. The figure of Christ, which occurs rarely, is present crucified on Kirk Michael 129 (101) (fig. 37), while a more elaborate crucifixion scene occurs on the Calf

---

49 Page 1995, 223.
50 Kermode 1994, 214; Page 1983, 138-9. A late ogham inscription was excavated by the television Time Team at the Speke, Braddan, keeill in 2006, but is not yet published.
51 Kermode 1994, 101.
52 Grandell 1988.

Fig. 39. The two sides of Andreas 128 (102). Left, Odin swallowed by Fenrir; right, Christ trampling the serpents. Surviving height: 35cm.

of Man slab, 61 (50) (fig. 35). The fish on Andreas 128 (102) (fig. 39) is in all likelihood a symbol for Christ, derived from a rendering of the first letters of Christ's name and title in Greek – ἰχθνς. The fish seems to identify the man carrying a cross and a book in the same scene as Christ, and it is conceivable that the snakes in the scene refer to a passage in Psalm 91, '... you shall step on asp and cobra, you shall tread safely on snake and serpent ...' The cock (a symbol of the Resurrection), most notably on Andreas 131 (103), (fig. 31), is probably Christian in its iconography, particularly when associated with a Crucifixion, as on Michael 129 (101), but may sometimes have a double meaning in that a cock also appears in Norse mythology as Gullinkambi, who wakes the gods at the end of the world.

A Christian message may also be read into the 'hart and hound' scenes found on a number of Manx crosses.[53] This motif, which depicts a dog attacking the back of a deer's neck, has its origin in the Roman world and was adapted into Christian iconography. It

---

53 E.g. Kermode 1994, pls. xlvii, liv and lv.

occurs on Pictish Christian sculpture and on Viking-age sculpture in northern England, and has a number of well-defined Christian meanings in the later Middle Ages.[54]

While the Christian imagery is obvious, there is another iconographic schema on The Manx Stones – the Scandinavian – which is equally obtrusive, but much more difficult of interpretation, although it does indicate the meeting of the two religions at the time of the conversion to Christianity. Such a juxtaposition of imagery is not uncommon in conversion periods in the Germanic world generally, and in some Scandinavian regions, including northern England. The Church – of necessity – was remarkably tolerant of the pagan religions of the north, while the unfocussed organisation of the pagans resulted in an easy syncretism at the time of Christianisation. Conversion in Man is likely to have been an individual and gradual process, not imposed from above by legislative decision after negotiation (as in Iceland *c.*1000), through diplomatic treaty (as in the

54 Bailey 1980, 72 *et passim*, discusses some of these meanings. See also Bailey 1996, 84-94, for a more thorough discussion of Christian and pagan iconographic syncretism.

Fig. 41. Stone from Ramsey, Maughold 122 (96). Scenes from the Sigurd cycle. On the other face of the stone is a pair of interlaced Jellinge-style animals. Surviving height:1.2m.

eastern parts of England in 878),[55] nor as the result of aggressive missionary endeavour, as in a later period in the Baltic states. The pagan incomers to the Island established themselves in an already Christian community; but, as has been seen by their apparent tolerance of the Christian burial rite, they do not seem to have attempted to convert the natives compulsorily to their own religion. Rather – again from the evidence of the burials and the crosses – they adopted Christianity in the first or second generation of their settlement.

In the Island the gradual process towards conversion is well demonstrated iconographically on the fragment from Andreas 128 (102) (fig. 39). The purpose of the scenes is clearly exegetic. On one face is the god Odin, with his attributes of spear and raven and with his foot in the jaws of the wolf, Fenrir, in clear apposition to the stance of what I have interpreted as Christ on the other face. This is clearly a representation of a scene from the battle of the gods and giants at Ragnarǫk, which encompasses the death of Odin, when the world comes to an end with the promise that halls will rise where the noble live radiantly on. The relevance of the coming of Christ, as expressed on the other side of the cross, is obvious – the old world comes to an end, and Christ comes as harbinger of a new and better world as prophesied in the Old Testament. The idea of the heroic hall is paralleled by the Christian

---

55 *Anglo-Saxon Chronicle, s.a., 878.*

idea of paradise. This would make a lot of sense to a newly converted – or about to be converted – audience.

Kermode in his great book on the Manx crosses interpreted many other scenes on the basis of his reading of Norse mythology. Modern scholarship, however, is more cautious and critical.[56] Many scenes cannot now be interpreted, but some scenes from Norse mythology can be identified and are mostly concerned not with the pagan gods, but with the heroes and events of the Sigurd cycle.

Sigurd was a major hero of Norse mythology. His story survives in a number of sources and his history and identity were later inextricably mixed with the German hero, Siegfried, whose deeds are recounted in the *Nibelungenlied*. It is, however, the Norse cycle that is represented in the Isle of Man. The myths relevant to the scenes found on Manx sculpture are all summarised in Snorri Sturluson's *Edda*, which was written down in the early thirteenth century in Iceland and in the *Poetic Edda*, which was written down later in the century. One part of the story tells how Sigurd was incited by the smith Regin to obtain a hoard of gold protected by the dragon Fafnir (in reality Regin's estranged brother, who had turned himself into a serpent or dragon). Regin repaired and refashioned an old sword – called Gram – for Sigurd, who then went in search of the dragon. Having dug a pit, Sigurd hides in it and kills Fafnir with his sword as the dragon passes over the pit. Sigurd cuts out Fafnir's heart and cooks it. As Sigurd roasts the heart he burns his finger on it. Sigurd puts his finger in his mouth and, when the blood touches his tongue, he finds that he can understand the language of the birds, who tell him that Regin is treacherous and plans to kill him. Sigurd kills the sword-smith and takes Fafnir's gold away on his horse, Grani. Elements of this story appear in various guises on eleventh-century stone carving in Scandinavia, where it survives as a popular scene in wood-carving into the twelfth century.[57] Other representations of scenes from the Sigurd story appear on a cross at Halton, Lancashire,[58] and on four crosses in the Isle of Man – Jurby 119 (93), Malew 120 (94), Maughold 122 (96) and Andreas 121 (95). The Manx group of carvings, together with that from Halton, provide the earliest surviving representations of this cycle.

The clearest representation of Sigurd appears on Andreas 121 (fig. 40); on another stone (Malew 120, fig. 27) similar scenes are so badly worn that only a few details are clearly seen. In the lower panel, on the right-hand side on one face, Sigurd is seen slaying the dragon from below with the sword Gram, while in the upper panel he is shown roasting the dragon's heart on a spit and tasting its blood. The horse to the left at the top of the cross shaft is presumably Grani.

---

56 Margeson 1983.
57 E.g. Hohler 1999, ii, cat. no. 114, pl. 254.
58 Bailey 1980, fig. 15 and pp. 102ff.

Fig. 42. Fragment of memorial stone. Michael 123, showing a woman with trailing dress, carrying a staff. Height: 40cm.

A stone from Ramsey (Maughold 122 (96), fig. 41) has been convincingly shown to depict other parts of the Sigurd story.[59] At the base of the carving is a representation of the episode which begins the story as recounted in *Reginsmál*. As Otr (otter) bites into a salmon, the wicked god, Loki kills him. For this deed Loki was fined and the gold he paid formed the treasure Sigurd was to rescue from the dragon Fafnir. The horse, Grani, with the treasure-chest on its back appears in the middle of the field and at the top of the stone are smith's tools, presumably those used by Regin to refurbish the sword Gram.

The relationship between elements from the secular story of Sigurd and the death of a person commemorated by a Christian cross is obscure, but it may well refer to the heroic character of the person commemorated by the cross. In the words of the most

59 Margeson 1983, 101.

critical student of the iconography of the Manx crosses, 'The heroic deeds of Sigurðr and even representations of the gods (might they not have been seen as semi-historical antecedents of the well-to-do?) may have been intended to enhance the memory of the dead'.[60] Another possibility is that the idea of Christ as hero, as encountered occasionally in Anglo-Saxon literature,[61] is here paralleled by a legendary – but good – non-Christian hero. What is interesting is that there was an audience in the Island at that time which understood this iconography and a version of the stories which lay behind it; an iconography that in many instances was based on secular story-telling. Further, the fact that the story appears in a Christian context may imply that there was a background in sermons or biblical exegesis which does not survive in literature, but which implies a sophisticated approach to the problems of the overlap between paganism and Christianity, and between the two elements in the Island's population. The same scenes occur in totally Christian contexts in Norway on seven wooden church-portals of twelfth-century date; these have been much discussed,[62] but with no further resolution of their meaning other than that they are stories of heroes in an heroic society. These Norwegian examples may, however, also stem from the iconography of the conversion, which took place rather later in Norway than in Man, and the two series may have a common exegetic origin.

Many images on the Manx crosses cannot now be interpreted. This is particularly true of the frequently occurring animals and birds which appear, sometimes singly, and sometimes in hunting scenes; but it is also true of the human figures depicted (incidentally, no trace of animals which could be hunted has been found in the Island). What is one to make, for example, of the spear-carrying rider at the base of the large stone, Andreas 131 (103) (fig. 31)? In this case it cannot represent the person commemorated, who was a woman; perhaps it represents her husband, Sandulf the Black, who raised the cross-slab and symbolised himself in a semi-heroic role as a hunter of the animals which crowd the side panels of the two faces of the cross.[63] One might ask whether the harpist on Michael 130 (104) is David, but if so who then are the other figures – clerics? – and why are they juxtaposed with an image of the 'hart and hound' motif?[64] These scenes have not yet been interpreted.

Women are less frequently found on the stones and are no easier to interpret. The figure of a woman carrying a staff on the fragment from Kirk Michael 123 (fig. 43) and a woman with the similar long trailing dress on Jurby 127 (99) are curiously paralleled in a number of ninth- and tenth-century contexts in Scandinavia, from which they

60 Ibid., 105; Bailey 1980, 124-5 makes some syncretic suggestions.
61 Cf. The late ninth-century poem, *The Dream of the Rood*, line 39, '...þa geong Hæleð, þæt wæs God ælmihtig...'[...the young hero, that was almighty God...].
62 Hohler, 1999, ii, 22-3, summarises these discussions.
63 Kermode 1994, pl. 53.
64 Ibid. pl.54.

must have been derived.[65] In Scandinavia, where similarly dressed women often carry drinking-horns, they have often been interpreted as 'Valkyries', the warlike female attendants of Odin in Valhalla, but they might rather be related to the *vǫlur* – 'staff-bearers' or peripatetic sorceresses.[66]

The wider context

The obvious and strong Scandinavian roots of the art and inscriptions of the Manx crosses have been indicated. Less clear is the ornamental relationship with other sculpture in the British Isles. While the main influences in Manx sculpture – both ornamentally and in terms of the runes – clearly come from Norway, that of the contemporary surviving sculpture of the Western Isles (while also clearly related to Norway) may reflect in some slight fashion – chiefly in the runes – Manx prototypes. The runic inscription on an early eleventh-century recumbent slab from Iona is related to the Manx series.[67] The ornament on the stone from Cilla Bharra (Kilbar), Barra,[68] however, while related to stones of the Manx series, is a pale reflection of them; the inscription is both in style and language closer to Scandinavian models. The runic-inscribed fragment from Inchmarnock, Bute,[69] on the other hand, is more closely related to the Manx stones. On this basis it is likely that these three stones are secondary to, and probably derivative from, the Manx series.[70]

The sculpture of northern Wales echoes some elements of the ornament of the Manx Viking-age crosses.[71] There is, however, no parallel to the Manx ornamental tradition in any of the sculpture of Ireland. The earlier Scandinavian styles (Borre, Jellinge and Mammen) are encountered there, but in other media – bone, wood, manuscript illumination, and so on – and, more importantly, they are rare (unlike the later Ringerike and Urnes styles). It is to be remembered, however, that Irish ornamental elements in the Island during the Viking Age are demonstrated on the Calf of Man crucifix (p. 72-4), which has no distinctive Scandinavian element.

It is in England that the most significant parallels to the earliest elements of Manx sculptural art – the Borre style – are found. But the meaning of their occurrence there is

---

65 E.g. Wilson 1995, figs. 38, 46-8.
66 Cf. Price 2002, 112-6.
67 Liestøl 1983.
68 Fisher, 2001, 106-8.
69 Ibid., 79.
70 The Iona 'ship stone', Graham-Campbell and Batey 1998, fig. 13.2, is sometimes related to the Manx series, but is perhaps closer to the north-west English series; see, for example, Halton, Collingwood 1927, fig. 191.
71 E.g. Penmon, Anglesey, Nash-Williams 1950, pl. xxxii; Redknap 2000, 88-93; Edwards 1999.

unclear. It has been shown above that there is a close relationship between the material found in the Viking graves in north-west England and the Isle of Man in the early years of the tenth century, when both areas were settled by Scandinavian invaders. There is also a concordance between the Manx and north English sculptural traditions. The Borre ring-chain and the plaited foliate tendril seen on Gautr's cross at Kirk Michael and elsewhere on the Island, are closely paralleled in England' where they appear on Anglo-Viking sculpture in north-west England and in the Aire and Wharfe valleys in western Yorkshire.[72] Interlace of the heads of a number of Manx crosses (similar to that on Gautr's cross) is found in rather more corrupt form in northern England, and it is therefore likely that the Manx crosses were the inspiration for such detail and for others.[73] Dating is difficult. Bailey, in dealing with the Cumbrian sculpture, recognises this and has written, '… it seems unlikely that sculpture showing the impact of Scandinavian-derived art can pre-date *c.* 920'.[74] If the Manx sculpture were earlier, it would be difficult to reconcile its date with the rest of the archaeological evidence. The beginning of the second quarter of the tenth century would, however, be a sensible median date for the start of both the Manx and Cumbrian series.

The grave-finds and the sculpture, then, provide a reasonable chronological horizon for the earliest Norse settlement of Man in the period at the very end of the ninth century, and for the conversion of the incomers to Christianity within the succeeding generation. But the stories told by the stones have far wider implications. They tell of mixed marriages (perhaps indicating a comparatively peaceful conclusion to a bloody settlement). They reflect what seems to be the relaxed attitude of both sectors of the population to the conversion. This is demonstrated by the use of iconography of both pagan and Christian origin; an iconography which is also seen in a less concentrated form in the Scandinavianised north-west England, with which the Island clearly had close ties. The sculptured stones indicate that there was a comparatively affluent population on Man in the tenth century and demonstrate by their ornament and inscriptions how major cultural influences had their origin in Norway and how, as with the Gautr stone, the indigenous strata of society were moving away from their origins. Tenth-century cultural relations with the rest of the British Isles outside the Irish Sea region (Scandinavianised north-west of England, Anglesey, Ireland and south-west Scotland) are, as expressed in ornament, only dimly perceived.

---

72 Cf. Bailey 1980, 216-22.
73 The only Cumbrian element claimed by Bailey from the Isle of Man is the so-called 'Stafford knot' which appears on a cross from Kirk Braddan and on a number of crosses in Cumbria, ibid., 222 and fig. 63.
74 Bailey and Cramp 1988, 26.

The pattern of settlement

The people

The Viking settlers of the Island took over and occupied land previously farmed by the local Manx population. The seizure was almost certainly brutal and probably bloody. The native Manx were presumably ousted from their homes, and reduced in most cases to slavery or little better, while the incomers, as is demonstrated by their burial-mounds and the linguistic and place-name evidence (below, p. 100-3), became dominant.

In discussing the structure of the initial settlement of Vikings in Man, the question of immigrant numbers could have been all important, but unfortunately will probably never be resolved. An estimate of an initial four-hundred settlers has already been mentioned; but this is little more than a guess. Further, the evidence for the presence or otherwise of women settlers is tenuous. It is noteworthy that no specifically female grave-goods of Scandinavian character (other than beads) have been found in the Island. This is in distinct contrast to the situation in the other lands around the Irish Sea and in the Northern Isles, where women's graves (though not found in great numbers) frequently include jewellery undoubtedly made in Norway. That being said, the rite of burial accompanied by grave-goods is of Scandinavian origin, and, while there are few furnished female graves in the Island, those that have been found would suggest that, even if they were of Scandinavian origin, the women had not retained the ethnic costume of the North (of which the distinctive jewellery was an integral part). A similar, if slightly modified, picture may be seen in the male burials, where non-Scandinavian grave-goods outnumber those from Scandinavia, which could suggest that these were the graves of people who had already been settled in the Irish Sea region or in western Scotland, and who had had time to furnish themselves with more local pieces of equipment.

If it is assumed that the majority of the original Viking settlers in Man came from other parts of the Irish Sea region; it may well be that the new settlers either already had wives and families drawn from these regions or had absorbed at least some cultural traits from them. If, further, there was a preponderance of male settlers who were two or more generations away from their original homelands, it is likely that they would have sought marriage with the local women if there were insufficient women within their own community. The Manx memorial stones referring to women would seem to illustrate this process. These inscriptions, and others which record male Celtic names, emphasise that it was not only local women who became integrated in the dominant community.

Whatever the ethnic origins of the people commemorating or commemorated by the stones, whether they were men or women, the language of the land-owning class was, as indicated by the memorial stones, Old West Norse.

The inscriptions are written in a reasonably pure form of the Norse language. Page has pointed to grammatical imprecision in the inscriptions of the earliest Manx stones, which, he hazards, 'may … (as some have assumed) … give evidence of a breakdown, even as early as the tenth century, of the strict system of accidence [i.e.inflection] in Old Norse such as might be expected if that language was being used in a community of mixed Norse-Celtic speakers'.[1] Others before Page had proposed a similar situation, assuming a widespread bilingualism,[2] which is an attractive theory, particularly by parallel with the widespread use of a later form of Manx in the post-medieval period when the official language was English. An eleventh-century ogham inscription in Gaelic from the Speke keeil site, Braddan, may be a small indicator of this bilingualism.[3] Barnes, however, perhaps makes too much of the so-called 'breakdown' of strict accidence in the inscriptions, but does point out that nobody has thus proposed that a pidgin language developed, perhaps because 'later Manx Gaelic shows no effect of such a development'.[4] It would seem likely that early Manx Gaelic survived as a separate language alongside Norse until Man came briefly under Scottish control, when it was re-formed into a version of the Manx Gaelic known today. Norse apparently disappeared at this time (late thirteenth century). If this picture is generally true, it would have been the richer elements of society in the Viking Age who spoke Norse and imposed it upon the Island (as witness the place-names, discussed below). A poorer element, survivors of the original population, spoke Manx, which continued as an 'underground' language throughout the Norse period and, changing with the centuries, continued in that mode until the nineteenth century. As will be shown below, Norse place-names – so strongly represented in the Island – seem, with few exceptions, to have driven out the names given to places by the native population, a factor which is not easily explicable, especially since at some time in the Middle Ages many of the place-names were renewed in Gaelic mode. The one element left out of this academic discussion is the possible presence of the English language in the Isle of Man. Traces of it exist before the Viking Age,[5] and it seems reasonable to suppose that English was present in some form as a minority language during the Viking Age, although the strength of its linguistic influence cannot now be calculated. Further, English and Norse belong to the same language group and might well have been mutually comprehensible, while Gaelic had to be learned as a

---

1 Page 1983, 138.
2 Megaw 1978, 288.
3 Televised Time Team excavation 2006.
4 Barnes 1993, 76.
5 Cf. the two Anglo-Saxon runic inscriptions from Maughold, Page 1999, 137, 143-4.

separate language. English would, therefore, easily have replaced Norse in the Middle Ages. Latin, of course, remained the official language of the Church.

The social structure of the inhabitants of Man in the Viking Age – other than the fact that there was a ruler or king – can only be surmised on the basis of archaeological evidence, which reveals little beyond the presence of a wealthy upper class of Scandinavian incomers, some of whom intermarried with locals. The land-owning head of a household, if having a military past – as presumably did the men in the mound burials – would probably be described in Old Norse as a *þegn* (cognate with English 'thane'). A landowner who had not borne arms, yet was a free man, was perhaps known as a *hauldr*. While it may be interesting to speculate on such terminology, it may be irrelevant in relation to Man, particularly as it is based on legal definitions of social structure in medieval Scandinavia which may not have pertained in the Viking Age. The new major landowners were probably already socially well-established by the time of their arrival in Man; they would have brought free retainers and wives with them, and almost certainly brought their slaves. The presence of dependent free men on the Island cannot be documented, but they would have been a necessary adjunct, as armed men, of any initial take-over of land. Such men may, when the situation had calmed down, have been settled on secondary farms and their presence might be represented by the swords found in pre-existing graveyards (p. 51).

The fate of the ousted pre-Viking landowners and their families is not known. A few of the more powerful may have clung on, but it is likely that most lost their farms and were reduced in social circumstances as hired men and women; many almost certainly became slaves, an endemic status in the Irish Sea region,[6] as in much of northern Europe. We have seen how one woman – presumably a slave – was sacrificed in the Viking burial-mound at Ballateare. The Scandinavians were certainly involved in the trade, a major source of supply being Ireland. People carried off in raids were sold, some to the North. Rich Vikings would tend to be slave-owners.[7] Christianity should have signalled the end of slavery; but the fact that the institution was so frequently condemned by the church only emphasises that it was difficult to eradicate.

Many Viking-age slaves were women; indeed, a woman's lot in Man, particularly if she were of Manx birth, would not (as in Scandinavia) be far removed from slavery.[8] There were, however, among the incomers rich, wealthy free women (some were probably even landowners); the richly furnished grave on St. Patrick's Isle (fig. 20) was probably of such a person, and there may also have been rich women of native Manx origin. The names of seven women – one foster-mother, one daughter and five

---

6 Pelteret 1981, 110-11.
7 Ó Corráin 1997, 96. For slaves and the slave-trade in Scandinavia, see Foote and Wilson 1970, 65-78; *KLNM. s.v. 'Træl'*.
8 For women in the Viking Age see Jesch 1991.

wives (above p. 77) – are recorded on the memorial stones. The people commemorated may have been from wealthy families, and it may also be assumed that even some of the women with Celtic names remembered in the runic inscriptions would have been free women. Malmury, for example, on the Kirk Michael stone discussed above (p. 77), was the daughter of a Gael, married to a man with a Norse name. But whether she came from Man or from another Celtic-speaking – presumably Irish or Hebridean – area is difficult to say. Whether these Celtic women were forced into marriage with the incomers is not known, but it is not unlikely; in a similar situation the chronicler Frutolf, for example, records that, after the Norman Conquest, English women were dragooned into marriage with the newcomers.[9]

The arguments outlined above refer chiefly to the first century of the Scandinavian presence in the Island, but they suggest that integration was reasonably achievable and that it would continue and increase.

Settlements and forts

With the exception of Dublin and Waterford, York and the other towns of the English Danelaw, some major settlement sites in the Northern Isles of Scotland and a scatter of sites in the Western Isles, archaeological traces of domestic Viking settlement in the British Isles are exiguous. The Isle of Man, however, does provide some evidence – however minimal – of rural settlement, economy and subsistence, which adds colour to the rather more substantial data outlined in the previous chapters.

Where did the Viking incomers live? Geomorphological and palynological studies of the landscape and vegetation of the Island have revealed little. Studies of the Manx wetlands in recent years – unsurprisingly – show little more than that they were more extensive in the Viking Age, while it has also been suggested that there was much more activity on the uplands in this period than might have been thought.

Although much discussed, there is no concrete evidence of the political and legal structure of land-holding in the Island in the Viking Age. Our knowledge of land-holding in Man in the late medieval period is, however, reasonably robust and may be cautiously used in relation to the Viking Age. At the base of the pyramid in the later Middle Ages were a series of family estates known as 'quarterlands', which generally comprised an area of between 20 and 73ha (most normally about 36.5ha) and occupied the best farmland of the lowlands. Notionally these quarterlands were grouped together in units of four (with some variation) to form a 'treen', which later acted as a tax unit,

---

9 Schmale and Schmale-Ott 1972, 78.

but may originally have had another function.[10] By the fifteenth century Man had been divided for legal purposes into six *sheadings*; the sheadings also controlled land not held by the major quarterland farms – the mountains and bogs. Attempts have been made to carry the first two of these late medieval divisions back into the Viking Age, and it has even been suggested that the treens may have their roots in the pre-Norse period.[11] There is no documentary evidence of the land-holding structure of the Island in the Viking Age. Further, there is no hard evidence to support the statement occasionally advanced (by sometimes rather tenuous parallel with the situation in the Northern and Western Isles, where land assessment was based on *pennylands* and *ouncelands*) that the late medieval Manx *treen* system – with its quarterland subdivisions – had its origin in the pre-Viking period. The other administrative element of the medieval period – the parish – did not exist in the Viking Age, although it may be assumed that some parishes were centred on the field churches (keeils) which were important elements in the structure of many treens.

Many years ago it was suggested that the grave-mounds discussed in the previous chapter:

> ...may be the monuments of the first generation of settlers only, if we may judge by the distribution of the burial mounds in the north-western parish of Jurby. There six isolated burial mounds are distributed evenly among the same number of 'quarterland' estates: as if each of the original land-takers had been laid to rest singly, with full pagan ritual, at or near the highest point of his own lands.[12]

The proven Viking-age mounds were indeed placed on what in medieval times were certainly the major farms.[13] It should be noted, however, that this pattern is found only in the parish of Jurby. Other mounds and major single graves – like those at Balladoole, Arbory, or Knock y Doonee in Andreas – are almost certainly related in similar fashion to quarterland farms, and are on the highest point of their estates, but may not reflect the distribution pattern of the Jurby graves. Indeed, Balladoole is placed on the edge of a communal pre-existing cemetery and Knock y Doonee is sited near a keeil, which conceivably had a pre-existing sacral history as a burial site. Any suggestion

---

10 The term is first recorded in the late 15th- /early 16th-century Manx Traditional Ballad, Draskau, stanza 14. Crawford 2007, 225, postulates that it came to Man in the 10th or 11th century. See also Ditchburn and Hudson 2007, 383. It may be derived from the Gaelic *tír unga* [an ounce of land], equivalent to its tax value as an ounce of silver.

11 For literature, see Reilly 1988, who would also take the quarterland divisions back beyond the Viking Age; Moore 1999, 179.

12 Megaw and Megaw 1950, 146.

13 For a map of the mounds see Megaw 1976, fig. 3. A modified version is in Megaw 1978, 282.

of a correlation between Viking burial mounds and quarterland farms must, then, be treated with caution. There is no ready explanation of this difference, which might easily depend on social, religious, topographical or geomorphological factors. As to the mounds themselves, it has been suggested above that they are statements of power, set in the landscape to emphasize a new regime and the establishment of a new hierarchy of land-holding, parallel to the re-naming of places and estates by incomers.

If, however, the correlation of mounds and quarterlands is accepted (and it is based on fragile evidence in a small region of the Island), it would imply that the quarterlands and the larger multiple estates (treens) could have been established either at the time of the Viking settlement or, possibly, before the Viking Age.[14]

This is discussed further in the next chapter. For the present, the date and origin of the formal systems of land-holding in the Island awaits radical re-examination; current arguments are based on little more than guesswork, however intelligent. It is not even clear how the incomers held their land either at the time of settlement or later. When, for example, did land become the gift of a central authority – a king or chief?

The archaeological evidence for the houses of the Vikings is more robust in that physical remains of the Norse settlement have been excavated and published. But the available data provided is uneven, particularly in that only one dwelling-house – that on St Patrick's Isle – has been excavated in what are truly the lowlands, and that dates from the late eleventh or early twelfth century – the very end of the Viking Age.[15] Nor has any farm site of Viking-age date been excavated in the most fertile parts of the Island, on either the southern or the northern plain. Further no evidence of field systems of this period has been recognised, although traces of ploughing were found under the burial mound at Cronk Moar.[16] This said, a number of promontory forts around the coast were occupied in the Viking Age, as well as a slightly anomalous series of superimposed buildings – at Vowlan, at Ramsey – which the excavator suggested belonged to a promontory fort, an interpretation that has recently been questioned.[17]

Forts

Promontory forts on sea-cliffs are well known in Ireland and Wales where they seem to have been occupied, abandoned and re-occupied at all periods from the Iron Age to the late medieval period.[18] A promontory fort of similar size to these examples is

---

14 Megaw 1976, 20. See also Reilly 1988, 113-9, who has ignored the fact that many mounds are of Neolithic or Bronze-Age date; Moore 1999, and Williams, G. forthcoming.
15 Freke 2002, 136-9.
16 Bersu and Wilson 1966, fig. 39.
17 Bersu 1949; Johnson, 1997-9, 51-2.
18 E.g. Norman and St Joseph 1969, 78 and fig. 45. Raftery 2005, 165, gives a critical summary of the dating evidence for the Irish forts. See also Edwards 2005, 254-5.

Fig. 43. Cronk ny Merriu, Santon, from the air. The promontory fort is in the foreground.

Burroo Ned, overlooking the Sound between the main island and the Calf of Man (fig. 3). Most promontory forts on the Island, however, were much smaller, cutting off a headland overlooking the sea by means of a bank and external ditch (fig. 43). Within the enclosed area was erected a house or series of houses. Bersu recognised twenty-one such sites, but some are doubtful.[19] As elsewhere in the Irish Sea region, the Manx forts are multi-period; Close ny Chollagh, Malew, (fig. 44) for example, certainly had pre-Viking-age levels; three circular houses were excavated below the vestigial remains of a rectangular house which was probably of Viking-age date.[20] Other forts – Cass ny Hawin[21] and Cronk ny Merriu,[22] Santon (fig. 43) – have revealed aisled houses of what are presumed to be of Viking form with lateral benches, a central hearth and opposed

19 Bersu 1949, fig. 8.
20 Gelling 1957.
21 Gelling 1959.
22 Gelling 1952.

Fig. 44. The bank and ditch of Close ny Chollagh, Arbory. Set on a headland, there is a landing place in the bay beyond, which in the Middle Ages was the site of a beach market.

doors at one end (fig. 45).[23] Excavation has produced little material, probably because rubbish was thrown over the cliff, while wind erosion and driving rain removed the rest. At Cass ny Hawin, however, there were a few finds. A spearhead and part of a pair of shears (while not accurately datable) would not be inconsistent with Viking-age typology, although the pottery seems to be of thirteenth-century date.[24] This latter element would be in line with the multi-period nature of these sites, which is also indicated by the find of a halfpenny of Edward I (*c.*1280) immediately below the turf near the north-east corner of the fort at Cronk ny Merriu.

The forts are set in very exposed positions – it would sometimes be difficult to walk upright to them in a high wind. They are now reached by cliff paths, but the original topography would have allowed access across fields. It is difficult to see how they could have been used as permanent domestic settlement sites. It also seems unlikely that they were taken over by the earliest Viking settlers to protect themselves from the indigenous population. Most stand above a beach, some of which were used in the

---

23 Doonan 2001, 42-4, suggests that Hango Hill, on the edge of Castletown, may represent another fort. Geophysically surveyed and minimally excavated, an irregular oval hearth has been dated by the radiocarbon method to between 898 and 1017. The evidence is thin, and its position is such that it may not happily be compared to the other forts, with the exception of the possible fort at Vowlan. Excavation might confirm this hypothesis.

24 Barton 1999, 228.

Fig. 45. Cronk ny Merriu. The interior of the building within the promontory-fort as excavated, showing the remains of benches along the walls (a typical feature of Norse houses).

medieval period as periodic market-places; the forts, perhaps occupied seasonally, or at least temporarily, could thus well have had a function in protecting traders or the boats of the locals. It has been suggested they could have been used collectively as a protective look-out system against inroads from the sea.[25] This attractive theory does not explain why some of them at least date from the pre-Norse period, unless their function had originally been similar. This said, the dating of these sites is based on very shaky evidence, but the form of the rectangular houses found within them chimes well with Viking-age houses elsewhere. It might well be, as has been suggested, that the houses in some of the forts preserve the form and internal layout of the traditional Viking building until well into the medieval period.[26] The long period during which the forts were occupied (even if only on a temporary basis) might suggest that their usage changed through the many centuries revealed by excavation.

As a pendant to this discussion, it should be mentioned that a substantial Viking-age rampart was excavated on St. Patrick's Isle. It is dated, 'not earlier than the tenth century

---

25 Cubbon, 1983, 18-19. Collins 2003, 338, suggested on the basis of no evidence or parallel whatsoever that they, 'may have been utilised…as slave-holding quarters [for] onward transit and beach-side trade'.

26 Johnson 1997-9, 55. See also idem. 2002, 63-80.

and the layers above it are not earlier than the mid-eleventh century.[27] Its function is uncertain, but it is clearly the forerunner of the series of military works on the islet which culminated in the building of the imposing medieval castle with its curtain wall. It may indeed indicate that the islet was a seat of power; a suggestion reinforced by the presence on the site of a series of ecclesiastical buildings in the late Viking Age.

Farmsteads

If the promontory forts remain an enigma, the few traces of farm-buildings datable to the Viking Age are remarkable only for their rarity. One site, at the Braaid, Marown (fig. 46), is, however, of importance in that it seems to show continuity between the pre-Viking-age inhabitants of the Isle of Man and the incomers – the only example in the Island. This continuity of use is not, however, a unique phenomenon in the Viking world, it is also seen in Orkney and Shetland, for example;[28] but such a clear statement of continuity on a single farm is rarely encountered. The Braaid site, which lies on the 130m contour within the arable land of a slowly rising valley, survives as a series of upright stones which looked so megalithic that it was for many years classified as a prehistoric ceremonial site. This was questioned by Fleur and Dunlop in 1942, who suggested that two features might belong to the Viking Age – an hypothesis confirmed by exploratory re-excavation in 1963.[29]

The site is multi-period. It consists of a pre-Norse round-house and two other buildings; one is rectangular (16.5 x 6m) and has transverse divisions which suggest that it was a byre. The walls are of stone rubble and the remains of the stalls consist of upright stones. More surprising is the main house, which is internally 20m x 8m at its widest point. The walls were curved and the gable-ends now show no traces of the structure that filled them, although it is assumed that it must have been turf or timber (timber gable-ends are familiar in Iceland to this day). The entrance was presumably through one or both of the gable-ends, as there is no sign of an entrance in the long walls. Little remains of the internal features of the building, although there are hints of lateral benches. The surface of the floor has eroded away and no trace of a fireplace was found. The walls of the house were used after it became derelict to enclose a number of simple stone and turf shelters. Through the middle of the site runs a sluggish stream which today gives a boggy quality to the ground.

The propinquity of the round-house and the other buildings suggests that the site had a continuous history as a farmstead through the pre-Norse period into the Viking Age – the incomers presumably introducing into the Island a new architectural fashion,

27 Freke 2002, 135.
28 Graham-Campbell and Batey 1995, *passim*; Hamilton 1956.
29 Fleure and Dunlop 1942, 53. Gelling 1964.

Fig. 46. Aerial view of the Braaid, Marown. The walls of a Viking-type house with curved walls and traces of benches along them is in the foreground. Behind it is a byre, to the left of which are the remains of a pre-Norse round-house.

the rectangular building. Such a sequence was repeated many times in the Scottish islands, most notably in Orkney, at Buckquoy and Birsay, where a series of rather more irregular 'round-houses' were replaced by ones of rectangular form.[30] Houses with curved sides are known in northern Europe from the fourth century AD onwards – in Scandinavia, Germany, Holland and England – and are seen in their most developed form in tenth-century Denmark.[31] In Britain buildings of this form occur sporadically, although rectangular buildings are generally the norm.[32] The external appearance of such curved-walled houses is most clearly demonstrated sculpturally in northern England and southern Scotland, where the tenth-century 'hog-back' tombstones imitate not only the curved walls seen at the Braaid, but also the curved roof-ridge implicit in the form.[33]

30 Graham-Campbell and Batey 1998, 160-5 and references cited, pp. 274-5.
31 Olsen and Schmidt 1977, 139-48.
32 Rahtz 1976, 88 (for England); for Scotland, e.g. Graham-Campbell and Batey 1998, fig. 9.4.
33 Conveniently summarised in their architectural context by Schmidt 1994, 137-57.

A house as large as that at the Braaid, would, in the Viking West, have had internal transverse partitions, perhaps dividing its ends from the main room with its central fire. The detached byre, while unremarkable in a western Viking context, adds to the impression that the farmstead was at the centre of a sizeable economic unit, belonging presumably to an important Norse incomer. We shall never know why the site was abandoned, although it might simply be because the yard became too boggy for comfort. Nor can we say whether a new site was found for the farmstead's economic successor. The Braaid, though substantial, was not in later times recognised as a quarterland. The place-name is first mentioned in 1704 (*Brade*) as 'intack',[34] a term usually reserved for moor or common land.

Johnson has pointed out that the Braaid, while not strictly an upland site, is situated on the edge of, or actually in, what must have been marginal land. 'A tempting solution,' he suggests, 'might be to see the farmstead as being deliberately set on, or close to, the point where arable infield downslope gave way to grazing outfield nearer the hill lands.' He further suggests that it might even have degraded to such an extent during the Viking occupation that its status may ultimately have sunk to that of a shieling, represented at a late stage by the small huts found inside the large house.[35]

Another farm complex, at Doarlish Cashen, Patrick (fig. 47), was certainly placed on marginal land. This rather eroded site, 210m above sea level, was excavated in 1970.[36] While its buildings are much smaller than those at the Braaid, this seems to be more substantial than the normal Manx shieling sites of later (thirteenth-century) date, especially since it is associated with a field system. Further, its main building, a rectangular house which measured 7 × 3m internally, has a layout of typically Norse form. It has opposing doors towards one end, the doorways defining a screen which cuts off the end of the building. The main room had lateral benches and the floor was spread with the debris of a hearth. Associated with the main dwelling were a number of subsidiary buildings, one of which has been interpreted as a grain-drying kiln built on the remains of an earlier structure.[37] There is doubt as to whether the interpretation of this structure is correct on the good grounds that it faces south-west – the direction of the prevailing wind – which would provide too much heat for such a purpose. Could it represent a cooking oven?[38] The other structures are not so easy either to identify or to date. Doarlish Cashen was a permanent settlement of the Norse period, even though it may have been almost entirely dedicated to hill grazing and may have been abandoned to be replaced in the medieval period as a shieling. Whether or not settlement on marginal

---

34 Broderick 2000, 175.
35 Johnson 1997-9, 57.
36 Gelling 1970.
37 Ibid., fig. 31.
38 Cf, for example, Schmidt 1994, fig. 17.

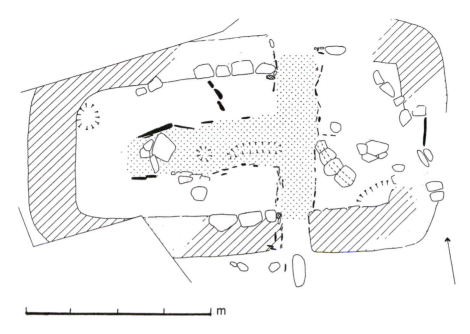

Fig. 47. Plan of the main building at Doarlish Cashen, Patrick. The stippled area indicates a charcoal spread from a presumed fireplace in the main room. (After Gelling 1970).

land is indicative of land shortage cannot yet be answered, but the implication is that Norse settlement in the Isle of Man was fairly dense. Recent, and as yet unpublished, work on field boundaries – while based on minimal evidence – would suggest that land was farmed to the limit. In investigating cuts through fourteen field boundaries broken by the laying of a gas pipe-line in 2002/3, a rescue survey by the University of Liverpool Centre for Manx Studies recovered a number of samples capable of radiocarbon dating. One of these, at Twelve Shares on Beary Mountain (no. 6 in the survey) – which lies at the upper limit of the later intack – was dated to the eleventh century (990±65BP). Such a result must be treated with extreme caution, but it possibly implies farming at the very margin of utilisable land at the end of the Viking Age.

The uplands were also presumably used to graze sheep and cattle, presumably seasonally, and a number of shieling sites have been surveyed and examined in recent years.[39] Surveys in the 1960s identified fifty shielings, but only two, Injebreck and Block Eary, have been properly excavated. At the latter site, on the north side of Snaefell,[40] the find of a single coin of Stephen (dated 1135-41+) was at least significant and points to the possibility that sheep were moved to summer pasture on the uplands as early as the the twelfth century and no doubt in the Viking Age. Block Eary was clearly in

39 Johnson 1997-9; Johnson 1999.
40 Gelling 1962-3.

use over a long period of time; five huts of stone and turf with brushwood roofs were excavated, all had collapsed on a number of occasions and been repaired. Internal and external hearths were found; there may even be evidence of cheese-making and there are perhaps indications of growing and drying grain. Most shieling sites consist of a number of single-celled huts, sometimes with an enclosure or sheep-fold. In one case, for example, at a rather complicated site known as Upper Rheast, in Druidale, the foundations of more substantial buildings might suggest a more permanent settlement, and the possibility that it dates back to the Viking Age cannot be ruled out.[41] It has been persuasively argued that these seasonal upland sites were continuously in use from the Viking Age into the Middle Ages, although there is as yet no excavated material to support this theory.[42]

In effect, the sites discussed above provide us with the only surviving physical evidence of the agricultural and defensive settlements of the Viking Age in the Island – and the dating and interpretation of some of them are based on shaky suppositions. None represents a major farm of the type which can be associated with the quarterland farms of the medieval period. In order to test the theory that quarterland farms had an origin in the Viking Age, it has been suggested that excavation should be carried out on the site of known quarterland farms; this has not been done, but the proposition remains valid.[43] Exploratory excavation at the quarterland farm of Kerrowdhoo, Bride,[44] has produced thirteenth- or fourteenth- century pottery and the farm may have an earlier ancestry. It will, however, be difficult to achieve significant evidence of lowland farms of the Viking Age without more systematic investigation of a major site.

Place-names and settlement

Place-name evidence illuminates to some extent the settlement-pattern of the Viking Age in the Island (fig. 48).[45] It is assumed that the spoken language of the Island in the pre-Norse period belonged either to the Brythonic branch of the Gaelic languages (either from Wales or Cumbria) or to the Goedelic of Ireland. The evidence is confusing since both languages appear in the pre-Viking inscriptions, but in numbers that are statistically useless. The language which emerges in the thirteenth century, at the end of the Norse hegemony, is Goedelic, which suggests that it might have survived through the Viking Age and beyond as the base language (see below p. 136). It is clear that Norse was the language of communication among the wealthier elements of Manx

41 Johnson 1999, 158 and fig. 5.
42 Johnson 1997-9, 64-5.
43 Wilson 1974, 16.
44 Davey 1995.
45 The best summary continues to be Fellows-Jensen 1983. See most recently idem. 2002 and 2001-3.

Fig. 48. Finger post. The names terminating in -by are Norse. Ramsey is a Norse construction (hrams-á – i.e. 'garlic river'). Ballaugh is a Manx Gaelic name, meaning 'farm of the lough'.

society in the Viking Age (see p. 88f). At the same time, the Celtic personal-names on the memorial stones demonstrate that there was, at least in the tenth century, an underlying element of the population which probably used a Gaelic language, which in the eleventh century was perhaps strengthened, or at least kept alive, by continuous contact with both western Scotland and Ireland.[46]

Although this substratum of Gaelic language apparently remained throughout the Norse period, it is clear that Scandinavian was dominant and was much used in constructing place-names, while arguably retaining some pre-Norse elements.[47] Despite

46 Thomson 1983 and 2007. Below p. 136.
47 For the survival of place-name elements see Fellows-Jensen, forthcoming.

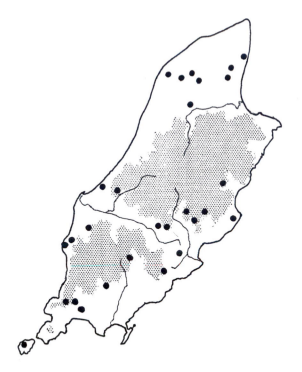

Fig. 49. Distribution of place-names terminating in -bý; a clear indication of Norse settlement. Land over 400ft (122m) is stippled. (Based on Fellows-Jensen 1983, fig. 1.)

the continuity of Gaelic language and settlement, only three certain pre-Norse place-names survive in the Island – the name *Man* itself, the name of the parish of *Rushen* and the name *Douglas*, the present-day capital (but see p. 136-7). As the Scandinavian language became dominant, Scandinavian place-name elements become reasonably common in major settlement names, such as those of the treens (above p. 88f). Generally, the Scandinavian names cannot be dated, although there may be a few exceptions. There is, for example, a single putative indication of pagan settlement – *Aust* – which could have developed from the compound **hof-staðir*, a name well attested in Iceland, which could mean something like 'the settlement of the temple', but it is more likely that it had to do with the place's economic or political significance.

Many of the names of Scandinavian origin are topographical; they describe the features of the landscape important to the settlers. In order of frequency they include -*vík* ('bay', as in Fleshwick), -*dalr* ('valley', as in Foxdale), -*fell* ('hill', as in Lambsfell), -*nes* ('point' or 'headland', as in Langness) and so on. Names based on the type of settlement are rarer. Elements of the termination –*staðir* (as –*st(aðir)* in Leodest), known in about a dozen places, may represent, as in Norway and the Northern Isles, an early, but secondary, settlement unit separated from its original estate – perhaps given by a person of high status to one of his military supporters. The termination -*bý* (as in Jurby) is thought to have a similar sense to -*staðir*, but to be of Danish origin, probably arriving in Man through the north of England (fig. 49). For a short time Fellows-Jensen argued

CHAPTER 4

that several names with a *-bý* termination could have been introduced into the Island by followers of the Stanleys, granted the lordship of Man in the early fifteenth century, who based them on names familiar in their Lancashire homeland. She did, however, make it clear that quite a few of them – like Tosaby and Sulby (which are recorded in late thirteenth-century documents) – are of pre-Stanley date. Now, however, it has been generally agreed to abandon the idea of a Stanley origin of these names, while stressing that 'the recorded name-forms have in many cases been subject to English influence'.[48] All this said, many of the Scandinavian place-name elements in the Isle of Man must have been introduced in the Viking Age. Many more were presumably lost after the Norse hegemony had failed and farms and settlements were re-named by owners of different linguistic groups.

The basic economy

Knowledge of the basic economy of Man in the Viking Age can only be founded on supposition. The soil was good and medieval writers praise the quality of its produce. Archaeology reveals little evidence of the utilisation of the land, although plough-marks have been noted beneath the mound at Cronk Moar (p. 36) – these were presumably made with a simple ard (i.e. a plough which broke the surface of the ground, but had no mould-board to turn a furrow). This was probably hauled by an ox. Other tools would include spades, and various forms of harvesting implements, sickles and leaf-hooks – all well-known in the Norse world – but of these only two sickles of possible Viking-age date have been found on the Island, at Cronk yn How[49] and at Ronaldsway.[50] Although a great deal of evidence of cultivated grain has been found from the prehistoric levels on St. Patrick's Isle, there is no published sample of Viking-age date from this or any other Viking site.

As there were no roads on the Island, only a few tracks, it is probable that sledges of various forms were used to drag loads, as they were until the eighteenth century.[51] The native Manx horse is now extinct, having died out in the nineteenth century. They were in effect small ponies, no bigger than thirteen hands,[52] the same size as that found in the Knock y Doonee mound.[53] They would have been ideal to draw the primitive sledges of the period, which would have consisted of two shafts fastened by cross-members, the out-turned members of the shafts being dragged along the ground. It is possible that they were used with two-wheeled carts, but this is unlikely as even wheelbarrows

---

48 Fellows-Jensen 2001, later modified in Fellows-Jensen 2001-3, 435.
49 Bruce and Cubbon 1930, figs. 16, 17.
50 Neely 1940, fig. 4,11.
51 Megaw 1943, fig. on p. 100.
52 Megaw 1943; Kavanagh 1988, 103.
53 Kermode 1930, 132.

were unknown until about 1700. In general, wheeled vehicles did not replace sledges and pack-animals until the mid- to late eighteenth century.[54] Riding horses were used only by the rich – they were status symbols, expensive of upkeep – but they could presumably have also been used for draught purposes.

Domestic animals are poorly documented. Burnt bones of ox, horse, sheep and dog were recovered from the Ballateare mound-burial, while on St. Patrick's Isle a small amount of bones of sheep and cattle were recovered, as were a few bones of a pig in eighth- to twelfth-century contexts.[55] This result is hardly surprising, save the fact that three times as many (180) bones of cattle were found as compared to sheep (so ubiquitous in the Island nowadays). The only known byre of this period was found at the Braaid (fig. 46), where the animal-stall divisions are still visible.

In the Isle of Man agriculture has always been practised alongside fishing and, although a great number of fish bones were excavated on St Patrick's Isle, only one small deposit was dated to the Viking Age. It must, however, be assumed that fish was eaten widely on the Island; the small boats from the Balladoole and Knock y Doonee burials would have been ideal for offshore fishing in good weather; indeed, a lead fishing-line sinker was found in the Knock y Doonee grave. As today, there would have been a good amount of line-fishing from the rocks and beaches throughout the Island, and such delicacies as crab and lobster could have been harvested by line-fishing or gathered under rocks on the shore. Oysters were more common around the Island's shores in the Viking Age and their shells were found in some numbers throughout the medieval levels on St. Patrick's Isle.[56] Sea-birds were presumably also netted for food (they were a major export in later times), and their eggs would have been gathered in season. Game-birds (including wild duck) and hare were also caught for the pot and would supplement such domesticated birds as chicken, goose and duck.

54 Quayle 1794, 21.
55 Freke 2002, 248-9.
56 Ibid., 262.

CHAPTER 5

Economy, politics and the Church

In the previous chapters the Viking settlement of the Isle of Man has been examined on the basis of archaeological and place-name evidence assembled by professionals and amateurs over a period of more than a century. Compared with other areas of the British Isles this evidence is richer, more varied and – because of the geographical constriction of a comparatively small Island – more focussed than most. In turning to the political and administrative structure which affected and may have controlled this settlement, we struggle to interpret shadowy references in written and semi-historical sources and – often controversial – conclusions based on theoretical parallels with better documented, but still shadowy, systems elsewhere in the western reaches of the British Isles.

Hoards and coinage

One body of material, however, provides an indication both of the Island's comparative economic strength in the tenth and eleventh century, and even (at least in the eleventh century) an element of administrative sophistication. This is based on the interpretation of the hoards of precious metal – mostly silver (including many coins) – buried in the Viking Age and never, for whatever reasons, reclaimed by their original owners. Twenty-two Viking-age coin-hoards and four hoards without coins have been found in Man over the last 250 years.[1] One coinless hoard is unprovenanced, but may come from Balladoole, Arbory.[2] Of the hoards with coins, one poorly-documented hoard (probably from Kella, Lezayre) may be dated to the late ninth or early tenth century; all the others are dated between 960 and 1070. Another ill-documented hoard, found before 1785, may date from the late eleventh or early twelfth century. The richest hoard is from Ballaquayle (sometimes known as the 'Woodbourne' or 'Douglas' hoard) (fig. 50). Many of the coins in this hoard (of which there were perhaps as many as 370), and possibly some of the silver objects, went astray after it was found in 1894.[3] The surviving silver objects (without the coins) weigh about 1kg, and it has been calculated that it originally weighed between 2 and 3kg.[4] It also, unusually, contained a gold arm-ring which weighs 78g.[5]

---

1 An odd find, but worthy of mention, is a variant of a gold solidus of the Carolingian emperor Louis the Pious (814-40), found in Maughold churchyard in 1884; Blackburn 2007, 81.
2 Graham-Campbell and Sheehan 2003-5.
3 The most recent study of the coins in the hoard is Pagan 1981.
4 Collins 2003, ii.
5 Gold is rarely found in insular Viking contexts, but there is a suggestion that the Andreas hoard contained some gold objects; Blackburn 2007, 77.

Fig. 50. The Ballaquayle/Douglas hoard. Objects in the British Museum (other objects are in the Manx Museum).

In such finds the wealth of the Viking settlers and their successors is clearly confirmed. The rich burial customs of the original settlers demonstrate that this was not a poor community (at least insofar as its more important landholders were concerned). Its wealth is further emphasised by the elaborate – and fashionable – nature of the carved stone memorials of the Scandinavians after their conversion to Christianity, of a decorative quality which is in some cases as high as any in the Viking world.

The hoards represent a measure of the portable wealth of one section of the Island's society and of its ability to support – however fleetingly – a standard of living well above the subsistence level of most of its inhabitants. The contents of the hoards speak not only of internal wealth, but of foreign contacts and ultimately, through coins minted on the Island, of the power and administrative control of its rulers, elements at that time unknown in the rest of the British Isles outside England and Dublin.

There was, however, no monetary economy based on coins struck in Man until well into the eleventh century (and even then coins were minted for a short time only). Although the Manx lived on the fringes of the European economy; merchants and the more travelled members of society in the Island would have been familiar with coins which – minted to strict standards in Europe, Byzantium and the Arab world – circulated with some freedom in the Viking homelands and their settlements abroad. In Scandinavia coins were only minted from the beginning of the ninth century, but sporadically, and then only in a very limited number of centres. By no stretch of the

Fig. 51. Reconstructed scales from a grave at Ronaldsway. Only the balance-beam survives. This is of unusual form in that it has a series of nicks for a sliding weight, which is more common in the later medieval period. Its date could be disputed, but the object is clearly an indicator of the presence of a merchant on the site. Scale 2:3.

imagination can the Scandinavian economy be said to be based on coins minted at home, but they may well have used the foreign coins as a means of tender. The presence in the Isle of Man of five single-finds of silver coins which date to the second quarter of the tenth century (the period in which no hoards have been found), while only a small sample, is just significant enough to postulate the use of coin – as coin, not as bullion – in the Island before the deposition of the first hoards;[6] but whether it represents a stable and peaceful period of Manx history is a moot point.

Although barter was a significant element in the Viking trading economy – particularly at a local level – trade in an international context was often more sophisticated than the simple exchange of goods. The medium of much trade was silver (and very occasionally gold) coin and bullion, which was measured by weight on small scales carried by merchants (the balance arm of such a pair of scales – together with a lead weight – has been found at Ronaldsway; fig. 51). The bullion could consist of ingots, jewellery (either complete or cut-up pieces) or 'ring money' (see below). The silver was tested for purity with a sharp knife (the resulting marks of this primitive

6 Metcalf 1992, 101.

form of assay are known as 'nicks' or 'pecks'). Apart from the coins struck in the Island in the second quarter of the eleventh century, all the Viking-age coins found in Man were minted in other countries – primarily in England, either in the Anglo-Saxon kingdom or in the Scandinavian-controlled Danelaw; a few coins are of Continental origin, while an increasing number after *c*. 997 were minted on an Anglo-Saxon model by the Scandinavian rulers of Dublin. Interestingly, hoards containing coins which definitely date from the first thirty years of the tenth century are not found in Man,[7] which parallels the situation in Scotland. In northern England and Ireland on the other hand hoards of this period are quite common (there are about twenty in all).[8] This uneven distribution may well be due to the chaos caused by the expulsion of the Scandinavians from Dublin and the consequent instability in North Wales and north-west England to which areas they fled.

Minting of coins in western Europe in the period covered by this book was rigorously controlled by rulers, who withdrew coin series and re-issued them on a regular cyclical basis. The English coins were called pennies; 240 pennies made a pound. Pennies were not insignificant in value, a few coins could buy a pig. In the reign of King Æthelstan of England (924-39) a pig was valued at five pence, a cow at twenty pence, an ox at thirty pence and a good horse at 120 pence. As deals were done in such amounts it was important that the standard of the coin, by weight and silver content, should be maintained. There was, however, a reduction in weight as the cycle progressed. Coin weights, although strictly controlled, varied from cycle to cycle and from ruler to ruler, the heaviest being about 1.6g and the lightest 1g. This is particularly true after the reform of the English coinage (that most significant for Man) carried out by Edgar after 973-5, the king making all the profit by buying in the coin by weight and re-striking them by face value on a cycle of up to six years.[9] The cyclical re-minting thus makes it relatively easy to give an end date for the deposition of individual hoards, because of the absence of coins of a particular minting. In the Isle of Man such indications show that coin hoards were generally laid down between the 960s and the 1070s, with a break between the 990s and the 1030s (fig. 52). The earliest coin-hoard from Man, which is unprovenanced, dates to *c*. 955-60. Excluding this find, seven hoards date between *c*. 960 and *c*. 995, and, although this cannot be called a sophisticated statistical sample, it has led to the tentative suggestion that hoarding in Man seems to have started soon after the beginning of the expansion of the Dublin trade and the beginning of a more adventurous phase in the life of the Scandinavian settlers of the Island.[10] Man lay on the

---

7 Graham-Campbell 1983, fig. 3.
8 For a clear account of the English coinage see Dolley 1976; Metcalf 1980, 1981 1986. Cf. Blackburn and Pagan 1986. 294-5.
9 Jonsson 1987.
10 Graham-Campbell 1983, 72.

CHAPTER 5

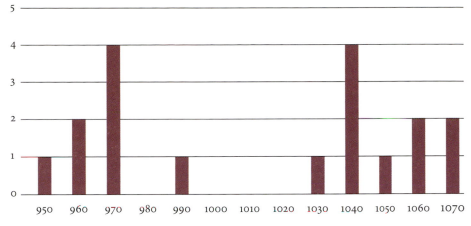

Fig. 52. Manx Viking-age hoards by decades.

main north/south trade-route from Scandinavia, through Orkney and the Western Isles of Scotland to England, through Chester and the Bristol Channel and through Dublin to the Continent. The hoards both by their content and distribution clearly reflect the use of this route; the Island hoards providing concrete evidence of the involvement of the Manx Vikings in this trade.

It is, however, possible that some of the wealth represented by the later hoards in this group may have been 'danegeld' obtained in England by Manx Scandinavians fighting on the side of the Norwegians or Danes. Such mercenaries had to be paid, and there is evidence in Swedish runic inscriptions (backed by the presence of a vast number of Anglo-Saxon coins deposited in Swedish hoards) of such payments for military service in England.[11] Further, the mid-eleventh-century hoards with their strong Irish content, while reflecting trouble in the Irish Sea area, might indicate similar payments for mercenary activities nearer home just as easily as hoards hidden against immediate attack.

After 990, no Manx hoards can be definitely dated before 1030 (Park Llewellyn, Maughold), but eleven hoards may be placed between the latter date and the 1070s, some of which contain coins which were almost certainly minted in the Isle of Man based on the Dublin style and standard. It is clear that Dublin was deeply influential in Man at this period, and it is perhaps significant that hoarding ends in the Isle of Man shortly after the arrival of a new king in 1079 – a king who may have had more local control over the Island. Politically Man seems to have turned northwards in the late eleventh century as a new Norse king established his hold on the Island (although he probably had his original power base in Ireland).

11 Jansson 1987, 77-9.

The hoards were deposited by people who either lived in Man or took refuge there – most probably the former.[12] They could have been laid down for any of a number of reasons: to protect wealth in time of trouble, for safe keeping at any time, or even (but almost certainly not in the Isle of Man) as ritual deposits to placate or thank the gods. They probably reflect tough and dangerous times. The safest place to keep portable valuables was to bury them in the earth, but the fact that they survive in such great numbers and were never reclaimed suggests that their owners and their families may well have suffered in the unruly events which took place in the tenth and eleventh centuries in the Irish Sea region. The dates of the early Manx coin hoards – between the 960s and the 990s – might suggest that the Island became a target for raids (or was subject to internal disorder) in the second half of the tenth century, in the period after the initial settlement when the settlers' wealth became common knowledge both inside and outside Man. It is impossible to say how the Manx Vikings of this period obtained their wealth – it may well have been through trading activity – but at this period the wealth demonstrated by these hoards might suggest that the settlers themselves had been involved in more aggressive activity, whether in a political or privateering sense, by allying themselves with the leaders of some of the many Scandinavian incursions in the region, or simply by acting as pirates.

So far as the tenth century is concerned, evidence for such incursions or activities is nugatory. There is perhaps a hint of a reaction against unruliness in the area by the very public way in which King Edgar demonstrated his power by bringing his fleet round to the Dee in 972, where a number of petty kings and chiefs in effect made submission to him, including Magnus, 'the king of many islands' (also described, as we have seen in a twelfth-century source, as 'chief of the pirates'). This act, by publicly stressing his power, showed that he was going to put up with no nonsense in the north-western parts of his kingdom.[13] The hoards of the 960s and 970s might have been hidden in a period of trouble which Edgar may have been attempting to quell by this display of power; an attempt which was short-lived as he died three years later. These troubles are reflected in the tenth-century raids on the north Welsh monasteries of Holyhead, Tywyn, Penmon and many more from 961 onwards.[14]

A Manx connection is suggested by a coin-hoard from the Castle Esplanade in Chester, dated c. 965, which, it has been said, 'looks like the property of Scots or Manx Norseman'[15] (although Ireland has been put forward as another alternative[16]). This

---

12 For the hoards, Collins 2003; Graham-Campbell, 1983. See also Cubbon 1997-9; Bornholdt, forthcoming.
13 See above, p. 22-3.
14 Davies 1990, 51.
15 Ibid., 54, following Graham-Campbell 1983, 70. A possible Dublin origin has also been suggested.
16 Graham-Campbell, forthcoming.

Fig. 53. Gold arm-ring and fragments of two silver neck-rings from Ballacamaish, Andreas. Approx. max. diam. of neck-ring 16cm.

suggestion is based on the fact that the make-up of the hoard is in no way similar to that of contemporary English hoards but is more closely comparable with the content of the earliest dated Manx hoard (that from Ballaqueeney, Rushen), which coincides almost exactly in date. This would suggest the sort of Manx activity that would be compatible with a period of turbulence in which the Manx played a part, and would relate to the deposition of the tenth-century hoards. The Chester hoard could then be seen as a fossil of trade or warlike activity between Man (or somewhere else in the Irish Sea region) and Chester, a major trading centre of north-west England.

The hoards themselves are intrinsically interesting. Some are quite simple; that from Ballacamaish, Andreas (fig. 53), for example, contained no coins, but included a neck-ring, which was complete but had been cut into three pieces. A fragment of a similar ring and a complete arm-ring were also found in the hoard.[17] The neck-ring, which is made of pairs of rods twisted together, has ends formed of hooks which engage with each other and are produced from beaten triangular end-plates ornamented with punch marks. It is of a mid- to late tenth-century western Norwegian type and is paralleled in an eleventh-century hoard from Halton Moor, Lancashire, but is little more than half its weight (102.8g).[18] The fragment of the second arm-ring is heavier and its four pairs of twisted rods are paralleled only in western Norway. The arm-ring, is also made of rods, twisted together with wires which are themselves twisted, the terminals finished with a sheet metal cap. Only one parallel is known, from a small hoard found at Port Glasgow, Renfrewshire.[19] The origin of the type is unknown.

Ballacamaish is fairly typical of the Manx hoards (with the exception of the Ballaquayle hoard which is discussed below) in that it contains material other than coins and consists exclusively of rings of one sort or another. The Ballacamaish rings were elaborate objects, made to be worn. The simple type of ring – formed of small plain penannular rods – found, for example, in the hoards from Ballaquayle (fig. 50, bottom left), West Nappin, Andreas, churchyard, and the Kirk Michael 1972/5 hoard – is however, classed as 'ring-money' or 'bullion-ring' (although there is no reason why they should not also have been worn).[20] The interpretation of this class of plain ring as a kind of currency is based on their simple form and on a study of their weight, which shows that they were produced (roughly) to a standard system based on a unit of 24 ± 0.8gm; the rings varying in weight between one and five units.[21] 'Ring-money' appears to have been developed in the first half of the tenth century and was clearly still in use until the end of the third quarter of the eleventh century, when the Kirk Michael hoard was laid down (c.1065). Although ring-money is clearly a Viking phenomenon, its main area of development and use seems to have been in Scandinavian Scotland, where over ninety complete rings and 200 fragments have been found. Its presence in the Island (which has produced twenty examples) seems relevant to continuing contacts with Scotland in the tenth and eleventh century.

17 Ibid., no 11.
18 Ibid., no. 4:2.
19 Graham-Campbell 1995, no.1, p. 95.
20 Another similar ring has recently been found on the Island.
21 'Ring-money' is most conveniently and thoroughly discussed by Graham-Campbell 1983, *passim* and 1995, 30. See also Graham-Campbell and Sheehan 2003-5. For metrology see Warner 1975-6, 141.

Another element of bullion is represented by ingots, roughly shaped in a sub-rectangular mould.[22] These are often cut into pieces, presumably to be traded by weight. A recently-found hoard from Glenfaba, its deposition dated by 464 coins to *c.* 1030, contained 25 ingots, of which thirteen are cut fragments.[23] Ingots otherwise are rare in the Island, although an example does occur in the Ballaquayle hoard, the most important of the Manx hoards (fig. 50).

Other bullion of non-monetary form is represented by the 'hack-silver' found, for example, in the Ballaquayle hoard. 'Hack-silver' is the technical term now used to describe silver – often derived from objects of personal adornment – which has been cut up and used as bullion, and traded on the basis of its weight. It is assumed that the smaller the pieces, the more frequently they have been exchanged in the course of trade. In the Ballaquayle hoard the pieces are quite large, suggesting that they had not been in circulation for any great length of time. The hoard also included several hundred coins, possibly as many as a thousand, (which allow its deposition to be dated *c.* 970).[24] An ingot, together with ring-money and hack-silver, emphasises the hoard's character as bullion. A number of items in the hoard had been tested for silver content by nicking with a knife – the familiar, if rough, form of Viking-age assay, mentioned above. Nicking is not very frequent in this hoard, again suggesting that the silver had been through few hands as bullion; but only seven items have no nicks, the average number of nicks is 2.5, and only one fragment has as many as six nicks.[25] Among the hack-silver in the Ballaquayle hoard is the fragment of a neck-ring made up of twisted wires, not unlike those found at Ballacamaish, save that its terminals were parallel-sided; similar neck-rings are found in western Norway.[26]

Fragments of other objects from Ballaquayle include three portions of 'ball-type' brooches, including the complete pin-head of a late variety of 'thistle brooch' in form and decoration paralleled in the Skaill, Orkney, hoard (above p. 70),[27] as indeed is the fragmentary ball-type pin-head (plain on one side, with an incised hexafoil on the other face). A complete pin bent into a loop has a type of socketed pin-head also found at Skaill and, associated with the very large ball-type brooches, in a hoard from Flusco Pike, Cumbria.[28] Among the complete objects are a finger-ring and two arm-rings. All the objects in the Ballaquayle hoard, save one, are of silver, but unusually the hoard also contains a gold object – an arm-ring. This is made of two twisted rods with a pair of twisted wires between them.

---

22 For ingots, see Kruse 1988.
23 Fox and Collins 2004.
24 Jonsson 1987, 206, identifies more than 405.
25 Graham-Campbell forthcoming,
26 Ibid.
27 Graham-Campbell 1995, pl. 13.
28 Graham-Campbell forthcoming, no.2:1.

Fig. 54. The Greeba, Marown, hoard of gold rings. Scale approx. 2:1.

In the words of James Graham-Campbell, 'The Ballaquayle hoard forms a classic example of a mixed Viking-age silver hoard, containing all four diagnostic elements in combination: coins, ingot(s), complete ornaments and hack-silver...'[29] The coins have a strong northern English character,[30] and many are bent (presumably to test their silver content). A good parallel is the similarly dated, if much larger, Skaill hoard from Orkney (which weighed more than 8.1kg, three times the weight of Ballaquayle; it also has a low proportion of nicking). Some, if not all, of its content had been used as bullion, but it cannot be categorised simply as a merchant's hoard. It has also been described as 'the accumulated capital of a Norse chieftain or leader, or of the most prominent family within the local community',[31] many of its contents having come from the Irish Sea region.

One remarkable find, which presumably represents a hoard, consists of three gold rings found more than fifteen years apart in the same field in Greeba, Marown (fig. 54).[32] One is a complete finger-ring made up of eight plaited rods, a type which is paralleled twice in Scotland.[33] A second finger-ring, hitherto unpublished, is made up of six

---

29 Graham-Campbell 1983, 69.
30 Metcalf 1992, 102.
31 Graham-Campbell 1995, 48.
32 Cubbon 1999-2001; Wilson 2001-3.
33 Graham-Campbell 1995, 127, 130 and pl. 50,1; 154 and pl. 73b.

twisted rods. The third is the fragment of an unusual ring (presumably a mount or collar) which has been cut into bullion in antiquity. It is decorated with a sophisticated animal in relief. The animal is of typical Ringerike style and must, therefore, date to the early eleventh century – a period when no silver hoards have been found in the Island. The pristine condition of both the twisted finger-ring and the animal-ornamented ring, and the interpretation of the latter as a failed casting, would suggest that this is a jeweller's hoard and that it could have been made in the Island (Ringerike ornament of this quality is, however, much produced in Ireland in this period and it is possible that the ring may have come as scrap from Dublin). This type of find is otherwise unknown from the Island in the Viking Age, but, as a representative of a luxury craft, it is a reflection of the wealth of the Island at this period and probably of the presence of craftsmen able to cater for more expensive tastes.

A Manx mint

A significant step in the study of the Manx hoards was the recognition by the late Michael Dolley that some of the coins in the Kirk Michael 1973/5 hoard were struck on the Island (fig. 55).[34] Re-examination of other finds has shown that such coins were not unique to this hoard. The coins were minted between c.1025 and c. 1065 (and possibly later). Some 63 Manx-made coins are known from this series, of which 31 come from seven hoards on the Island, and seven from East Baltic or Scandinavian hoards (the rest are unprovenanced). The Manx-minted coins in the Baltic presumably went there alongside a large number of other coins from the British Isles, either as danegeld or by way of trade. Further, it is significant that Manx-minted coins are not recorded in Irish contexts, particularly as the coins are modelled on those of the Dublin mint, themselves based on coins of the Anglo-Saxon series. There is thus good cause for them to be known to specialists as 'Hiberno-Manx'. Initially it seems that a single obverse die, or more probably a set of dies, came to the Isle of Man from Dublin and was used to strike the first coins before being abandoned to make way for locally produced dies, modelled on the original obverse die but gradually deteriorating in the quality of the ornament and the literacy of the legend. The coins are also an indication that there was some sort of coin-based economy in the Island at this time – even to the extent that Anglo-Saxon coins (of highly-trusted weight and silver content) were cut in half for minor transactions. The Manx coins were clearly produced in some quantity during their currency, but the production of the coins did not mean that coins from non-Manx mints were not circulating alongside them in the Island.

It is of interest that, while in England and Ireland there were strong active mints in the Viking Age, there were no mints in Scotland. The meaning of the Manx coinage is

---

34 See Bornholdt 1999 and forthcoming.

Fig. 55. Hiberno-Manx coins from the Kirk Michael hoard.

thus difficult to understand in any other terms than that there was a strong trade with the Island from the monetary-based economies. They also presumably represent an attempt by the ruler of Man to control an element of that trade.

Although market-places have not been found in Man, the presence of beach markets has been tentatively postulated. With a monetary economy based on local minting of coins, the likelihood of the existence of beach markets becomes more probable. That one such may have been at Ronaldsway is suggested below.

Marketing and trade

Nothing is known of the mechanics of trade in the Viking Age in Man, but certain inferences can be made. In order to control the import of coin (a royal privilege), but more importantly to supervise and tax trade, some system of oversight must have been in place. The creeks and beaches must have been monitored by representatives of the king in order to collect dues on traded items and to control the import of coin. The idea of beach markets was familiar around the Irish Sea in the Viking Age, the two most important examples at the beginning of the Viking Age being Meols on the River Dee and Whithorn in Galloway (fig. 4).[35] In Ireland the Vikings controlled the main international trade, not only of the Irish Sea, but also of the western Atlantic from Greenland to Spain, through the towns which they had founded and organised; particularly Dublin, but also Waterford, Wexford and Cork.

35 For Meols, Griffiths 1992, 2001 and Griffiths, Philpott and Egan 2007; for Whithorn, Hill 1997.

Fig. 56. Derbyhaven. Originally known as Ronaldsway, the sheltered beach (now behind a protective stone jetty, built 1842/3 on a rocky outcrop known as North Island) afforded a safe anchorage with a gently sloping beach as a landing place from prehistoric times. The Ronaldsway archaeological site is 200m beyond the trees on the right. A promontory fort (also not shown) is behind and to the left of the picture.

As there were no towns in the Island, trade was presumably carried out under supervision in a number of creeks and beach markets, places which later became well-recognised and were licensed by the lord. In the late eighteenth century the Commission of the English Parliament which examined the governance of the Isle of Man when the then Lord of Man, the Duke of Atholl, sold his regalities, listed four ports and twenty-three creeks.[36] Some of these latter – Poyll Vaaish, Port Santan, Port Soderick – and two of the ports – Derbyhaven and Ramsey – are overlooked by promontory forts (above p. 94-5) which may have had some monitoring function with regard to trade (a third, Peel, is overlooked by an eleventh-century defensive enclosure on St. Patrick's Isle, p. 95-6 above). One of these ports, Derbyhaven (fig. 56), was one of the best anchorages and beaches on the Island. Originally known as Ronaldsway, it is first mentioned in the *Manx Chronicle* in 1224, when it was able to accommodate a fleet of thirty-two ships.[37] But Ronaldsway has a much longer history. Under the present airport runway, a multi-period settlement and burial-site has been investigated which may have been the background to a landing-place and beach market. It is from a grave on this site that the beam of a coin-balance and a weight, of the type used by merchants, were excavated (fig. 51).[38]

36   Feltham 1798, 73.
37   Broderick 1979, f. 43r.
38   Skinner and Bruce-Mitford 1940. See Jondell 1974 for comparative balance material.

Ronaldsway is not an easy site to interpret, chiefly because the excavations were carried out some seventy years ago and were recorded only to the standards of the time.[39] Later interpretations have been less than convincing.[40] Finds span the period from the Bronze Age through to the medieval period. As well as the balance-beam, a small amount of Viking-age material was recovered from the site, but much must have been missed and their relation to the structures found is obscure. Nevertheless, this was clearly an important settlement-site (based on a significant pre-Viking Christian site). Its economy rested to some degree on the beach-market (demonstrated – so far as the Viking Age is concerned – by a few exotic bronze objects, glass beads, rivets and knives[41]), as well as on farming.

Land-holding

In considering other economic, political and ecclesiastical institutions of the Island which may have been introduced or modified in the Viking Age, land-holding presents the most difficult problem.[42] The suggestion discussed above that the quarterland system of tenure was already in use in the early period of Viking settlement and that the treen was known before the Viking Age, has a very fragile evidential base. Further, little is known of the pattern of power. We do not know how land was held, whether from a king or another chief, or where the centre of power was seated (but see below, p. 122). It is thus in effect impossible to discuss in any sensible fashion the structure of land-holding in Man in the Viking Age, and unwise to make statements about other units – the treen in particular, which seems in the Middle Ages to represent a multiple estate.[43] Debate concerning the date of the division of land into treens or into the main administrative divisions, the sheadings, is generally unconvincing in the absence of concrete evidence, although it has been argued that elements of the treen system could be of pre-Viking date.[44] A great deal is known about the structure of tenure and assessment in Man in the late Middle Ages (long after the Viking Age), but this does not mean that we should extrapolate backwards into an entirely different political situation without considerable caution. Rather we should take to heart the warning of Wendy Davies in discussing related problems in Wales:

---

39 Neely 1940.
40 Well recounted by Higgins 1999, 142-3.
41 E.g. Neely 1940, figs 2, 2; fig. 3, 1 and 2; fig. 4 25 and 26; pl. 2, 9 and 14.
42 See above, p. 91-2.
43 The most thorough examination of these problems were two papers, at one time enormously influential but now outdated: Marstrander, 1932, radically modified in idem. 1937. But see Megaw 1976, 34-7; C.E.Lowe in Morris 1983, 125-6; Reilly 1988, 20, 24-8; Moore 1999; Williams, G. 2007.
44 Most recently, but with every caution, by Moore 1999.

It is phenomenally unlikely, indeed incredible, that Welsh arrangements and institutions went unchanged for six centuries. I therefore regard it as unacceptable to suppose that the detail and the model that were appropriate to the twelfth and thirteenth centuries were equally appropriate to the sixth and seventh.[45]

'King of many islands'

We have no direct evidence of how Man was governed until long after the Viking Age, save that it was itself at varying times a kingdom or part of a kingdom, ruled by a 'king'. But even this term needs to be analysed. To Anglo-Saxon and medieval chroniclers the ruler of any independent entity could be seen as a 'king'. To the Norwegians of the early Middle Ages, however, he might not have been described in these terms. That there were kings in Norway in the tenth century is undoubted, but some of the most powerful people within the Norwegian sphere of influence, were semi-independent rulers (not kings) of whom the most clearly recognisable was the Earl of Orkney (who generally paid allegiance to the Norwegian king). This magnate was so strong that he was from time to time an important – indeed sometimes a dominant – player in armed struggles in the Irish Sea region, allying himself with the various leaders, including the ruler of Man. The term 'king' might then be an outside invention in references to the Island, but it is a term which we must accept for the sake of convenience in relation to the ruler of Man in the tenth and early eleventh century. Certainly the Irish of the late tenth century were familiar with a 'king of the islands of the foreigners' (*rí Innsi Gall*), which must surely be a forerunner of the later Kingdom of Man and the Isles (the Isle of Man and the Hebrides) (fig. 60). It may even be that the term 'king' was attached to this polity by Irish scribes.

Earlier in this book (p. 22-3) the 973 Anglo-Saxon reference to Maccus, [Magnús] 'King of many islands', was discussed. There was also a tradition in later Norse sagas of a king of the Isles, sometimes with reference to Man, and similar traditions occur in Welsh and Irish sources. There are enough hints in these sources to the Island's different alliances in the tenth and eleventh centuries, to suggest that the ruler of Man was sufficiently independent to play some sort of political game in the Irish Sea and among the Scottish Islands. That most rulers of Man were subject to another ruler is probable, but such a situation would be periodic and often nominal. The story of Edgar's progress on the Dee in 974 illustrates this supposition. Although Edgar had a fleet, its function was to protect his kingdom and supervise its trade, not to control the political entities of the seas which surrounded it. There is no evidence of an English political presence in the Island at this period, nor later in the Viking age. It is probable that it was never captured by the English in the Viking period (such an event would

---

45 Davies 1990, 82n.

surely have been recorded in the English sources), and the Edgar reference is the only surviving suggestion in any historical sources of any direct relationship in the Viking Age between England and what we must suppose to be Man and the Isles.

Certainly, when Man developed a coinage (a royal prerogative), it was one based on Dublin and not on an English mint, a fact which indicates the direction of the Island's economic and political interests, and one reflected in the complicated and mostly dimly-perceived accounts of the period in the Irish sources.[46] Complicated, because there is a period in the tenth and eleventh centuries, when interpretation of the occasional references to Man in the Irish annals leaves one floundering amid the activities of Irish rulers, who might, or might not, have had suzerainty over Man. These men invaded the Island, took tribute from it, or were even ruled from Man. There is in the Irish sources reference to a battle in Man in 987, and it seems that the Manx fought alongside Sigtryggr, king of Dublin, at the crucial battle of Clontarf in 1014. The emergence of Man in the late eleventh century as the documented centre of a wider polity would suggest that a kingdom of Man and the Isles had been established in the late tenth century, and that the reference to 'Maccus' as 'king of many islands', towards the end of Edgar's reign, may indeed be the first indication of the later political entity.

The Norse sagas – although written down at a much later date – suggest occasional alliances with, and dependence on, the powerful Earls of Orkney in the Viking Age and, by extension, with Norway itself.[47] The more contemporary Irish sources, on the other hand, show a continuous relationship from the late tenth century onwards with the Norwegian king, as well as with the Norse kings of Dublin and the over-kings of the Uliad of north-east Ireland.

The *Cronica Regum Manniae et Insularum* [the Chronicle of the kings of Man and the Isles],[48] the earliest entries in which were written down in the early thirteenth century, is – unsurprisingly, in view of its late date – singularly unhelpful about the Viking Age. The earliest recorded king of Man appears under the (corrected) year 1070, when Godred, the son of Sytric (Guðröðr, son of Sigtryggr) *rex mannie*, died and was succeeded by his son Fingal. Otherwise the first coherently recorded king is an Irishman, Godred Crovan (Guðröðr Crouan, popularly known in the Island, through later legend, as King Orry), who, according to the *Chronicle*, conquered the Island in 1079.[49] Godred was related to the various Norse dynasties of Ireland and had a power base in the Western Isles, which he extended to take in Dublin and probably

---

46 See Duffy forthcoming, chapter 1 and 2.
47 Crawford 1987, 66 and passim. See Davies 1990, 49-50, for a rather simplified excursion into this area.
48 Broderick 1979. See also Williams, B. 2007.
49 Broderick 1979, fols. 32-4.

Leinster, from which he was ejected in 1094, a year before his death in Islay. Whether the king was ordinarily resident in the Island is not revealed, but he is the king seen as the founder of the Manx dynasty by the chief author of the Manx *Chronicle*. The strategic position of the Island in the Irish Sea gave potential for the ruler of Man to be a major player – sometimes victor, sometimes vanquished – in the eleventh-century politics of the region.

The importance of the North Channel in controlling access to the Irish Sea from the north becomes of supreme significance with the continuing economic expansion of Dublin in the early eleventh century. It may well be that the Island became rich in this period, as suggested by the hoards and coinage. On the other hand the hoards may well reflect troubled times and the activities of the over-kings of the Uliad (basically Ulster), who were frequently involved in military expeditions against Man in order further to control access to the Irish Sea. In 1087, for example, the Uliad allied themselves with Dublin to attack Man, while in 1098 the Norwegian king Magnus Barelegs, having found Man in a wasted condition due to internal fighting, spent some time in putting it to rights, sending for timber from Galloway.

The Manx coinage throws an essential chink of light on the political structure of the Island in the second quarter of the eleventh century. The minting of coins – a symbol of power and a source of considerable revenue – was important to a ruler and the minting process would be closely controlled. No Manx king is named on the coins themselves, but then neither is any other king. Based on the style of the coins, authority for minting might initially have been derived from Ireland. On the other hand it is possible that a local Manx ruler acquired in some – perhaps devious – way a single obverse die, or more likely a number of dies, and struck coins on no authority but his own, depending on them being accepted as Irish or even as Manx coins. Thirteen coins have been found showing the use of such a transferred die. Minting was apparently so successful that, when the original dies wore out, new ones were made, perhaps in the Island itself if it had the necessary technology to produce the high-quality carbon steel for their manufacture. It is unusual for coins to be struck outside such centres of power as towns – so unusual indeed that many scholars at first resisted the thesis that these were indeed Manx coins because there was no town on the Island in the Viking Age. It has now been recognised that there are a number of other imitative, and probably unauthorised, coinages in the Irish Sea region with no obvious place of minting; The Manx coins are not, therefore, a unique phenomenon.[50] The coins themselves could well have provided propaganda backing for the legitimization of the status of the ruler of the Island, and one which would bring in a certain amount of revenue. They are also evidence of the existence of a monetary economy within Manx society, being presumably a significant element in the payment of tax, while their presence in hoards

---

50 Bornholdt 1999.

outside Man shows that they were also used internationally in trade or as payment for services.

The ruler of Man, however, would in all probability wish to control his own mint and he would almost certainly do this from a central power base, presumably that from which he would administer the Island and perhaps also most of the Hebrides. In the Middle Ages and later the power base tended to be based in Castle Rushen, round which the town of Castletown, the Island's first capital, was gradually formed. There is no evidence of any Viking-age structure on this site; but, if there was one, it would seem likely to have been overlain by the great castle itself. But there is another medieval castle in Man – on St Patrick's Isle – which has produced, as has been shown, a fair amount of archaeological evidence of a Viking presence, both religious and secular. It is at least plausible that this was the base of the king – his 'centre of power' – and, if so, it would be the natural place to establish a mint. Such a thesis provides at least a possible scenario for a royal seat.

Tynwald

An indication of the formal organisation of society is provided by the national assembly, Tynwald, which still exists and meets in the open air on Tynwald Hill in St. John's each year on old St. John's Day (fig. 57). It clearly has roots in the Scandinavian period. Tynwald Hill and the ceremonies which take place there are unique and internationally famous. The idea of an assembly under a name similar to 'Tynwald' is familiar in Scandinavia, and there seems no reason why the name should not have been introduced into the Island in the Viking Age. It presumably originally functioned, as did its Icelandic counterpart, Þingvellir, as a meeting to resolve disputes, to promulgate and execute laws, and to debate matters which would affect the whole community. Although an entry in the Manx *Chronicle* of between 1176 and 1187 has been said to imply the existence of Tynwald,[51] the text merely refers to '*omni mannensi populo*' [all the Manx people]. Tynwald is actually first mentioned as a place in the *Chronicle c.* 1228, when it appears as a battle site. The first and only record of the Tynwald assembly in the *Chronicle* occurs under the year 1237, '*congregatio totius Mannensis populi apud tingualla*' [an assembly of all the Manx people at Tynwald]. The word is of Norse origin – *þingvǫllr* – meaning 'assembly field' and place-names of the same construction as 'Tynwald' occur throughout the Viking world. There are, for example, at least eleven places in the British Isles where the name survives in one form or another – as *Dingwall, Thingwall, Tionga, Tingwal,* etc.[52] – others are known from Norway, Sweden and Denmark.[53] The earliest

---

51 Megaw and Megaw 1950, 166.
52 Fellows-Jensen 1993; Crawford 1987, 206-10.
53 Fellows-Jensen 1996.

CHAPTER 5

recorded mention of such a name occurs in the Greater Domesday Book of 1086 for the Cheshire place-name Thingwall.[54]

There are a number of parallel features in Scandinavia to the general physical appearance and function of the Tynwald site at St John's.[55] The earliest reference we have to a Scandinavian assembly – usually interpreted as a 'thing' although the source is Latin and that word is not used – occurs in the life of Ansgar (a missionary to the court of the *Svear* – the central Swedish kingdom – and later Archbishop of Hamburg-Bremen), written in 865-7 by his successor, Rimbert. The biographer describes the visit of Ansgar to the king of central Sweden at Birka and records 'an assembly of people, a stage having been arranged for a council on an open plain.' It was interrupted by torrential rain.[56] According to a thirteenth-century source for a tenth-century meeting, the Gula *thing* in western Norway met on a level field (like the plain of Tynwald).[57] A level area was also important at the site of the Icelandic assembly (the *Alþingi*) at Thingvellir, a feature which accurately reflects the name philologically.

The presence of the mound at Tynwald is another element which can be paralleled in Scandinavia – the king or *lǫgmaðr* (literally 'lawman'), who sat on it, being easily visible to the assembly. A number of *thing* sites in the Viking world are associated with mounds, either natural or artificial, some of which were burial mounds. An important example of such a local meeting-place is that at Aspa, Södermanland, Sweden, which even has a rune-stone close to a mound known as *Tingshögen* [the thing-mound], which records that, 'this stone stands in memory of Öpir on the thing-place...'.[58] Other examples of mounds associted with rune-stones, occur at Kjula, Södermanland,[59] and Anundshöj Seunda, Västmanland,[60] but few make such a strong topographical statement as that at St. John's does now. Some *thing* names, particularly in Denmark, are compounded with the element *haugr* [a mound]. This does not mean, however, that there was always a mound at such a place, but that it was merely a general term for a place of assembly.

It is unclear whether the Tynwald mound is based (as is sometimes stated) on a prehistoric burial site or is a later construction. Known nowadays as Tynwald Hill, its other name, Cronk Keeill Eoian (hill of John's chapel), refers to the site of the nearby

---

54 The spelling is erratic: *Tvigvelle* for *Tingwelle*. I am grateful to Gillian Fellows-Jensen for pointing this out to me.

55 Brink 2003 and 2004. I am grateful to Stefan Brink for allowing me to see these papers before publication. The most extensive survey of such institutions remains *KLNM s.v.* 'Ting'.

56 *Vita Ansgarii*, cap. 19. Brink 2004, 206, translates the word *scena* as 'hut', but the rain mentioned here makes it clear that it was an open-air stage or platform.

57 *Egils saga Skalla-Grímssonar,* cap. 56.

58 Jansson 1987, 124-5; Brink 2004, fig. 9.2.

59 Brink 2004, fig. 9.1.

60 Ibid, fig. 9.3. See this article for further references.

Fig. 57. The Tynwald ceremony c.1977. The Lieutenant-Governor sits on the top of the mound; on the lower tiers are the members of the legislature, clergy, local government representatives, coroners and Captains of Parishes. The titles of laws enacted in the previous year are read in Manx and English by the two deemsters (judges).

chapel, which has existed on or near the place at least since the Viking Age (a portion of a carved Viking cross with a runic inscription was found there). The site as it now appears consists of a mound, 25m in diameter at its base, rising in four steps to a height of 3.6m. To the west is the modern (1849) church of St John (which was built on the site of an earlier cruciform church). Linking the two is a banked processional way constructed in the early nineteenth century, some 190m long, which curves round the base of the hill and round three-quarters of the church. A Bronze-Age cist, presumably originally central to a mound is still to be seen in the hedge of the road to the east of the site. Geophysical and other surveys carried out in 1993 and 1996 have provided a putative history of the site. Tynwald Hill itself may be based on a mound of any date from the Neolithic to the Viking Age (fig. 58). At some undefined early period a rectangular enclosure – represented by short lengths of ditches found during the survey – possibly surrounded two mounds, of which the larger forms Tynwald Hill (the other is no longer visible). The earliest surviving plan of the site, dating from 1774, shows the mound and church at St John's set within a roughly rectangular sod wall with three entrances on the south side and one in the eastern corner.[61] The mound in some form then already existed in the Viking Age and, in the tenth century, the runic

---

61 Harrison 1871, fig. facing p. 12.

CHAPTER 5

stone was erected in the burial ground which underlies the present church and spreads out beyond it (Viking graves in the immediate vicinity are discussed above, p. 50-1). It is logical to suppose that a keeill was erected on the site of the present church in the tenth or eleventh century.

Many attempts have been made to find similar sites elsewhere in the British Isles. A parallel has been suggested between Tynwald Hill and Doomster Hill at Govan, just outside Glasgow, which was levelled at the beginning of the last century.[62] Doomster Hill was approximately 45m in diameter and about 5m high. Although it has now disappeared, an eighteenth-century engraving shows it as a flat-topped mound, with a wide step halfway up. Excavations have located its massive quarry ditch, some 8-10m across.[63] The size of its mound and ditch would suggest that it was a medieval motte, rather than a specially constructed *thing*-place, although the name implies a place of justice (it means 'judgement hill'). Other similar stepped mounds outside the Island have been compared to Tynwald.[64] Most are unconvincing. The Thingmount at Little Langdale, Cumbria, is a roughly rectangular-shaped mound (approx. 32×29m and 1.9m high) with rounded corners, a flat lozenge shaped top and three steps. First discussed in 1891, it was described as a 'Law Ting' and compared to Tynwald.[65] The name 'Thingmount' does not appear in the Westmorland volume of the English Place-Name Society (an institution peculiarly interested in meeting-places). It is certainly not an ancient name; it sounds and looks like a romantic conceit.[66] It is immediately adjacent to, and aligned with, an eighteenth-century farmhouse of some size belonging to a family of minor gentry (the Flemings of Rayrigg), from which it is now separated by a passageway of modern construction.[67] It is most probably specifically related to the house, perhaps as a terrace.

Stepped mounds at Lincluden Mote,[68] just outside Dumfries, and Maiden's Bower, North Yorkshire, are parts of motte-and-bailey fortifications of later construction. It is said that there are records of courts being held by Sir William (Black) Douglas in the late fourteenth century at the former site; the latter site was part of a fortification presumably built by William de Percy after the Norman Conquest.

---

62 Driscoll 1997.

63 Kelly 1994, 1-3, fig. 5. *Medieval Archaeology* 41, 1997, 320.

64 Most recently by Darvill 2004, 228.

65 Cowper 1891. The editor of the journal in which Cowper's article appears expresses (in a footnote, p. 6) a slight doubt as to its identity as a thing place. W. G. Collingwood, whose knowledge of Viking-age Cumbria was second to none at that time, writes in the introductory chapter to his novel *The Bondwomen* (1896) concerning meeting-places: 'But whether or no such a place was at Fellfoot in Little Langdale is not so certain'. Even he was sceptical!

66 Gillian Fellows-Jensen (personal communication) writes, '...Thingmount can hardly be a place-name. I would take the name to be the construction of an antiquary.'

67 Quartermaine and Krupa 1994.

68 Coles 1892-3, 118.

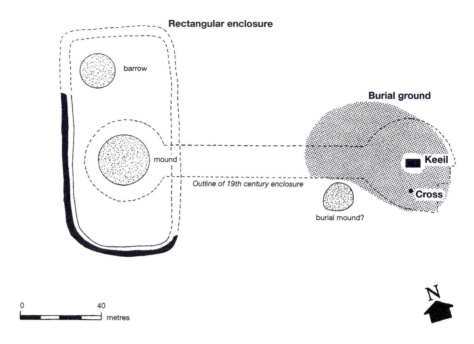

Fig. 58. *The Tynwald site. (After Darville 2004.)*

On the mound at St John's today, as from time immemorial, sit the representative of the Lord of Man (nowadays the Lieutenant-Governor) with his retinue and the bishop. Clergy, judges (in Manx 'deemsters') and members of the legislature sit on the lower tiers and members of the public observe the proceedings from outside the enclosure. This procedure is first recorded in a document of 1417, referred to as 'the Constitution of old time', drawn up for Sir John Stanley II (who succeeded to the Lordship of Man in 1414 and who was then to attend his first Tynwald ceremony). The document certainly refers back at least to the fourteenth century and gives some idea of the proceedings of the medieval ceremony, which presumably had its roots in a much earlier period:

> Our Doughtfull and Gratious Lord, – this is the Constitution of old Time, the which we have given in our Days, how yee should be governed on your Tynwald Day. First, you shall come thither in your Royal Array, as a King ought to do, by the Prerogatives and Royalties of the Land of Mann. And upon the Hill of Tynwald sitt in a Chaire covered with a Royall Cloath and cushions, and your visage into the east, and your Sword before you, holden with the Point upward; your Barrons in the third degree sitting beside you, and your beneficed Men and your Deemsters before you sitting; and your Clarkes, your Knights, Esquires and Yeoman about you in the third Degree … and the Commons to stand without the Circle of the Hill, with three Clearkes in Surplisses… Then the Chief Coroner, that is the Coroner of Glenfaba shall make Affence, upon Paine of Life and Lyme,

that noe Man make any Disturbance or Stirr in the Time of Tinwald, or any Murmur or
Rising in the King's Presence, upon Paine of Hanging and Drawing...[69]

This has enough echoes of practice at assemblies recorded elsewhere in medieval
Scandinavia to suggest that essentially the same procedure was carried out in the
Viking Age.

The Tynwald court was not always held at St John's; there are early records of it being
held at St. Luke's, Braddan, and – a special meeting – 'upon the Hill of Renurling'[70]
(Cronk Urley, Michael), but meetings at these places are mentioned only once. Darvill,
accepting some rather dubious philology of Kneen, has tried to identify sheading
assembly places by means of place-names.[71] None of them stand up to scrutiny in the
light of the modern place-name survey of the Island and the philological judgments
made there.

The Tynwald complex today is very different from what was there in the Viking
Age, but there can be little doubt that there was at that time an assembly of 'all the
Manx people' – whether at St. John's (which is more or less in the middle of the Island)
or elsewhere. Places of assembly in the open air are well documented from an early
period throughout Western Europe and fulfilled a variety of functions – as centres of
kingship, as places where kings were inaugurated or recognised, as assemblies for the
making or proclamation of laws, or for religious purposes.[72] The existence of such
assemblies in the Island before the arrival of the Scandinavian settlers, as suggested for
the Isle of Man by Broderick by parallel with the situation in other Celtic areas,[73] while
inherently probable, is undocumented. The claim of the modern Manx legislature to
have Scandinavian roots seems well founded.

The Church

Nothing is known of the organisation of the Church in the Viking Age. The Island was
Christian before the Vikings arrived, but none of the field churches (keeills) and only
a few graveyards have been identified as belonging to this period.[74] That there was a
monastic establishment at Maughold before the Viking Age is almost certain, while
Viking-age memorial stones found there demonstrate the site's continued use in some
sort of religious context. It is possible that the ecclesiastical elements discovered on St
Patrick's Isle also reflect the presence of a religious community there both before and

---

69 *Statutes of the Isle of Man*, 3-4.
70 *Statutes of the Isle of Man*, 1, 20.
71 Darvill 2004, 225-6.
72 Pantos and Semple 2004.
73 Broderick 2003.
74 See Bruce 1968, 71; Lowe in Morris 1983.

during the Viking Age, and it is even possible that there was a community at Ronaldsway. Rushen Abbey was not founded until *c.* 1134. It must be stressed that the Church in the pre-Viking Age in the Irish Sea region was neither uniform nor organised on the formal basis with which we are now accustomed as a result of the reforms of the tenth century. Davies has warned us of 'the myth of the Celtic Church'. While the organisation of the Church was tough and authoritarian, 'there was no single institutional structure encompassing all, or most, Celtic countries in the early middle ages'.[75]

It has often been assumed, based on little more than medieval propaganda concerning the deeds of St. Patrick and his followers, that the pre-Norse Church was modelled on, and linked to, its Irish counterpart. Whether this relationship existed and whether, if it did, it continued into the Viking Age is not documented, although the Calf of Man crucifixion slab (fig. 35) and the eleventh-century round tower on St. Patrick's Isle (fig. 59) are typical Irish forms,[76] and demonstrate contact with Ireland in the late Viking Age. Indeed, the presence of the round tower would suggest that (as in Ireland) St. Patrick's Isle at this period became – or was confirmed as – a monastic site. On the other hand the growing connection with the English Church, as demonstrated in the late eleventh century by the appointment of an English bishop (see below), should not tempt us too far towards an Irish model, where Dublin looked to Canterbury.

The administration of the Church during the Viking Age is also undocumented. It seems unlikely that the presumed pre-Norse hierarchy survived into the eleventh century,[77] although many Christian burial-grounds and the 'monastery' at Maughold seem to have a continuous history. A supplement to the *Manx Chronicle* names the first recorded bishop of the diocese, Roolwer (probably Old Norse 'Hrólfr'), who was appointed before Godred Crovan became king and was buried at Maughold.[78] It is significant that he had a Norse name and was appointed at about the same time as the first bishops of Orkney and Dublin, probably before 1074. As there were no territorial bishops in Ireland until this time it may be assumed that he was appointed from the North and that his diocese was some sort of primitive predecessor to the later diocese of Sodor and Man.[79] The next bishop had the Norman name, William, which may be accounted for by English influence in the Irish Sea region through either York or Canterbury. York was probably the archdiocese to which the kings of Man looked for the appointment of their bishops; not until 1154 did the bishopric became firmly attached to the archdiocese of Nidaros (Trondheim) in far-away central Norway. There is no mention of a monastic establishment in the Island in the Viking Age; and of the secular

---

75 Davies 1992, 14.
76 Lalor 1999, 96.
77 Woolf. forthcoming, considers a continuity from a pre-Norse diocese possible.
78 Broderick 1979, 50v.
79 For the early history of the bishopric, see Woolf forthcoming.

clergy only one is named – *Juan brist*, whose name appears on the two anomalous Maughold runic stones mentioned above (p. 78).

The question remains as to what the non-monastic clergy did, and who paid them. Although the parish system was not introduced into the Isle of Man until the twelfth century, some cemeteries, which became the graveyards of the later parish churches, were clearly, on the evidence of the sculptured stones, in use during the tenth century and probably earlier. Before the arrival of the Viking settlers most people were buried in cemeteries under lay control (Maughold seems to have been a monastic exception). It is clear that most, if not all, Manx keeills were first built in the late Viking Age, some on sites hallowed by prestigious burials marked by sculptured stone crosses decorated in Viking taste. At three sites, St Patrick's Isle, Speke and Keill Vael, the evidence demonstrates such a dating – to the late tenth or eleventh century – and this is likely to have been the general rule. A similar dating has been suggested for the churches of the Northern Isles and Wales.[80] The evidence for Ireland is more complicated, few if any ecclesiastical buildings can be dated before the tenth century, and those that do are of stone. It is, therefore, generally assumed that the early buildings were of timber, although no wooden church survives; an assumption backed by literary and even illustrative evidence.[81] Unfortunately there is no such evidence for Man, and the archaeological evidence – thin as it is – would seem to deny the presence of wooden buildings before the tenth century (even if timber was available on the Island, which seems doubtful).

It has almost been taken as axiomatic that keeills were important elements in the physical structure of treens, and that there was a keeill on every treen (but see above p. 91). This argument has become involved with many complicated discussions in relation to land-holding, land-divisions, and the organisation of the Church in a period before the creation of parishes. These discussions cannot be easily summarised,[82] suffice it to say in this context that, if there were a keeill to every treen, there would be nearly 170 of them on the Island, which seems an excessive number if one thinks of them in terms of modern churches – but not impossible if one thinks of them simply as chapels only serving burial-places.

The end of the Viking Age was presumably the period when the Church in Man, as in England,[83] began to take over burial rites and control the place of burial. There seems to have been a continuity of burial practice from the pre-Viking Age through to the post- Viking period on the few sites so far properly investigated. Although some of

---

80 Morris 1989. Jones 1992; Britnell 1990, has published an excellent example of a Welsh church and cemetery which tells a similar story, from Capel Maelog, Llandrindod Wells.
81 Stalley 2005, gives a good up-to-date summary of ecclesiastical buildings in Ireland,
82 A good summary is Moore 1999.
83 Blair 2005, 465.

Fig. 59. Round tower of Irish form, St Patrick's Isle.

the Viking-age dead on St Patrick's Isle were buried in wooden coffins or wood-lined graves, the use of lintel- (cist-) graves continued throughout the life of the cemetery, a rite that was probably due, it has been suggested, to the scarcity of timber on the Island.[84]

---

84 Freke 2002, 441.

In order to sanctify, and presumably control, existing burial sites, keeills would seem to have been built, often within the boundary ditch of a pre-existing cemetery, by local landowners and dedicated by the Church. They were simple single-cell structures,[85] served on an occasional basis by priests, who (following practices developing in England and elsewhere) would charge for their services at funerals, breaking with any previous informal (possibly lay) arrangements for burial. The keeills in the first instance may have been multi-purpose buildings, in which – as in Ireland – the visiting priest could live. It was presumably at this period that the buildings on some sites became in effect mother-churches served by priests. Some of these would have become the later parish churches.

A few keeill sites may have functioned as semi-monastic establishments – as hermitages or places of retreat. Lag ny Killey, Patrick, is often quoted in this context.[86] This interpretation has, rightly, been questioned;[87] but, when one looks at its isolated position, which is only theoretically on a route to the south of the Island (as anyone who has tried to walk southwards beyond it must concede), one is struck by its isolation – it would seem a site entirely suitable for a hermitage. The Irish parallels to this site are inescapable but perhaps overemphasised, as there are, in the view of many modern scholars, only a few confirmed isolated eremitical sites in Ireland.[88]

As the Viking Age comes to an end, Man begins to emerge – if only dimly at first – into the history of the political, economic and ecclesiastical structure of the British Isles.

85 Bersu 1970-2, 657; Morris 1983.
86 Lowe 1987.
87 Moore 1999, 172.
88 Edwards 1990, 116.

The legacy

After the Viking Age[1]

It has been demonstrated in the previous chapter that the end of the Viking Age did not mean the cessation of Scandinavian rule in Man. By the end of the eleventh century a kingdom, previously only hinted at in written sources, had been established – the Kingdom of Man and the Isles – which embraced both Man and most of the Western Isles of Scotland (fig. 60). The succeeding kings, until the Scottish take-over of the Island in 1266, were all descendants of Godred Crovan, who died in 1095. Relations with Dublin and Ulster were close, if not always of a friendly nature, and there was clearly an ongoing relationship both with the great earldom of Orkney and the now well-established kingdom of Norway, whose rulers claimed and achieved overlordship of Man and the Isles. The kingdom remained important politically and economically to Norway because of the sea-route which carried merchants from Norway to Dublin (which remained a major entrepôt with access to southern Englnd and France until Henry II's conquest of Ireland in 1171). Man and Dublin lived in an uneasy relationship until, in the 1150s, the rulers of Dublin and the leaders of an anti-Manx faction in the Western Isles formed an alliance. This led in 1156 to the division of the kingdom of Man and the Isles. Somerled, a Hebridean of mixed Gaelic and Norse descent with a power-base in Argyll, abandoned the Scottish mainland and briefly took over much of the northern element of the kingdom. Although the Manx and Norwegians managed to retain part of the Hebrides, their base was very insecure as Somerled's descendants continued to fight supporters of the Manx dynasty, a situation not really resolved until the final collapse of the Norse hegemony in this region in 1266.

Although disturbed conditions in Norway and rebellion in the Isles, coupled with the English conquest of Ireland, provided an opportunity for the Scots to increase their power in the west, they never seem to have capitalised on it. Man was still an important player in the region until 1266. Its rulers continued to hire its fleet to the highest bidder, as they had probably done for many years. In the early thirteenth century the Manx kings became – as mercenaries – more involved with the English, who needed to protect their shipping as they took over the lucrative Irish Sea trade. This engagement became so important that, under John (1199-1216), they became more or less subservient to

---

1 This section is largely based on Duffy forthcoming. See also Power 2005.

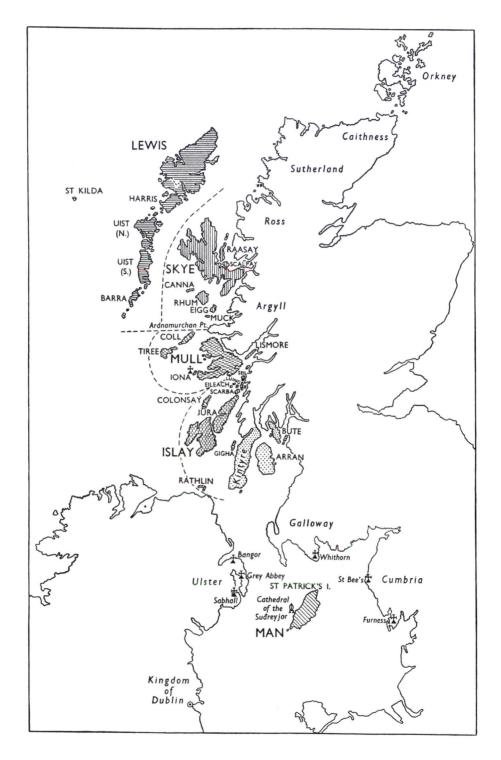

Fig. 60. The medieval kingdom of Man and the Isles. (After Megaw and Megaw 1950.)

the English Crown, although the Manx king still did homage and paid tribute to the Norwegian king. But external events were to overtake the Manx kingdom as the Scots and Norwegians fought to control the western seaways – most notably at the Battle of Largs in 1263. The Manx king, Magnús, was on the wrong (Norwegian) side and so, in 1266, under the terms of the Treaty of Perth, the Norwegian king Magnús Hákonarson ceded Man and the Hebrides to Alexander III of Scotland. Apart from an attempt by Magnús's illegitimate son, Godred, to seize the Manx throne in 1275 (a rebellion which was followed by great loss of life and serious plundering), Norwegian suzerainty of Man came to an end and the Lordship of Man became a possession of the heir to the Scottish Crown. In various guises and under various magnates it was to remain a garrisoned Scottish possession – often disputed in bloody fashion by the English Crown – until 1333 when Edward III of England declared that he had taken the Island into his own hands and passed the Lordship to William Montacute. The Lordship passed through many hands in the course of the fourteenth century until, in 1406, Henry IV settled it on Sir John Stanley, whose son consolidated what was to be a long association of the family (later Earls of Derby) as Lords of Man.

The Church was an important player in the story of Man in the post-Viking Age. The diocese of Sodor and Man was formally put under the authority of the archdiocese of Nidaros (modern Trondheim) in 1154, as a result of the organisational visitation to Norway by the English cardinal, Nicholas Breakespeare, as papal legate. This status was confirmed by the Treaty of Perth. The Manx diocese (separated from the bishopric of the Isles in 1387, but retaining its old title) in 1472 finally became part of the province of York, by Act of the English Parliament.

The Church clearly had, from an early stage, some relationship with England, emphasised by the appointment of a bishop with a Norman name to the see in the late eleventh century (above, p. 128). The mobility of the higher echelons of the ecclesiastical hierarchy at this period should not cause us to read too much into this single fact, for the next hundred years or more the bishops were generally also English, although a Manxman with a Scandinavian name, Hámundr, is recorded as bishop in the early twelfth century. A more tangible connection with England came with the foundation of Rushen Abbey from the newly-established Savignac (later Cistercian) monastery of Furness in Lancashire, c. 1134, by the Manx king Óláfr I. Furness's influence became increasingly strong in the administration of the Manx church; but after 1266, its influence waned, as the Scottish kings refused Furness's suggested nominations and submitted their own candidates to Nidaros.

A Norse inheritance

Until 1266 the Isle of Man had an unequivocal Norse character, owing allegiance to the Norwegian king, to whom its king paid tribute. It was presumably governed in harmony with Norse law and taxed on a Norse system. Its assembly, Tynwald, had parallels in the North and its Church after 1154 was under the formal control of the archdiocese of Nidaros.

Other influences are problematic – none more so than language.[2] It is clear that during the Viking Age Norse was used by the more important members of society – as witness the inscriptions. But there are faint traces, both before and during the Viking Age, of the presence of other languages – Gaelic, Latin and English. It is assumed that an undercurrent of Gaelic continued from the pre-Viking Age until the sixteenth century, when the Manx language first properly appears in documents. Gaelic personal names in Viking inscriptions give some credence to this view, but we have already noted two Anglo-Saxon runic inscriptions which almost certainly pre-date the Viking Age, and we may assume that there was some familiarity with English among the clergy of the twelfth century, when there was growing contact with English religious institutions. Latin would have been the means of literate communication through the medium of the Church. After the treaty of 1266 there was an influx of Scots into the Island, and the continuing contact with the Irish (as distinct from the Norse of Dublin) would also suggest that Common Gaelic was the most usual means of verbal communication. Norse was clearly abandoned, although a few Norse words, many to do with sailing and the sea, were taken into Manx. What cannot be measured is the relative importance of these various languages. Patronymics show the growing influx of a non-Manx population into the Island. Many important men, the Stevensons of Balladoole for example, came to Man in the service of the Scottish king and probably spoke some form of Scots or Scots-Gaelic The description of the Tynwald ceremony, quoted above, shows that by the early fifteenth century English was the official means of communication and record (with the occasional use of Latin). The developed Manx Gaelic presumably became the vernacular language of communication for most of the population until the nineteenth century, only to be revived by national enthusiasts in the last thirty years or so. But there is little early Manx literature – an historical poem of c. 1500 (written down c. 1700),[3] a few words in reports of law cases and basic religious texts (of which the earliest was the seventeenth-century translation of *The Book of Common Prayer*).

Place-names might be thought to help our understanding of the linguistic heritage of the Norse period in the Isle of Man, and there are, as has been shown, a fair number of place-names of high status which are of Scandinavian origin. While we cannot (as discussed above, p. 102) prove that any significant number of pre-Norse Gaelic place-names survive in the Island, opinion is growing among specialists in the subject that the incomers – like their cousins in England – took over existing names. On the other hand, a rare thirteenth-century Manx document, the Abbeyland Bounds of c.1280, lists many

---

2 Thomson forthcoming.
3 Draskau 2006.

Norse names which were to be replaced in the succeeding centuries by Gaelic or English names. Of the place-names recorded by the sixteenth century, the commonest are English constructions, probably, as in Ireland, formed by English administrators from Norse names, because such names 'were less lexically opaque to the English settlers'.[4] Some Norse names survived, partly because they were in a few cases remarkably similar to Norse names in the Earl of Derby's Lancashire – Crosby, for example. Manx Gaelic names are notoriously difficult to date; for example, the most common Gaelic name for a settlement is *baile*, as in Ballahot. Only one such name is mentioned in the Abbeyland Bounds – Ballasalla – but while there is a suggestion that some other names with this element survived from the pre-Viking Age, most – Ballafletcher, for example – are clearly much later in date, being compounded from English personal names. Names of Norse origin are striking survivals of the Scandinavian presence in the Island.

The House of Keys, today the elected assembly of the Isle of Man, is another Norse element that clearly survived the loss of the Western Isles to Scotland. Today it has twenty-four members, a number which was recorded in 1422 in answering questions put to the Deemsters and Keys by Sir John Stanley II: 'xxiij free Houlders, viz. viij in the Out Isles, and xvj in your land of Mann, and that was in King Orreyes days'.[5] The Keys were an important part of the governing structure of the Isle of Man, collectively known as Tynwald.

Tynwald is of course the most potent survival of the Norse period in Man, and its later description as a 'court' indicates its legal function which is enshrined, as has been shown (p. 126), in the 'Constitution of old Time'. Manx law in the Middle Ages was customary and unwritten. In the submission of 1422, it is stated that '… as to the Writeing of Laws, there was never any written since King Orreyes Days, but in the Time of Michael Blundell [the first Stanley Governor], that we have Knowledge of'.[6] It is interesting that this clause refers to King Orry (Godred Crovan), the late eleventh-century Norse King of Man, for he was seen as the founding father of Manx law, a proposition reflected in the earliest surviving poem in Manx, from *c.* 1500.[7] The laws were unwritten, and the Deemsters preserved the customary law without recourse to a jury, unless they felt the need for one. This law, known as 'brest law' (i.e. kept in the Deemsters' breast), was finally strengthened, in the face of increasingly despotic claims by the Earls of Derby, in an Act of Settlement of the English Parliament which was confirmed by the Keys in 1704. It was on the basis of the Isle of Man as an ancient independent kingdom founded in their Scandinavian past, with its own laws, that the Manx defended its separation from England. Ultimately it is this which supports the

---

4 Fellows-Jensen forthcoming.
5 *Statutes of the Isle of Man*, 11.
6 Ibid., loc. cit.
7 Draskau 2006, stanza 25.

qualified independence and prosperous state of the Isle of Man today, a status most recently confirmed and strengthened by the MacDermott Commission of 1959.[8]

The visual remains of the Norse period in Man, from the early burial mounds and the carved crosses to the great keep of Castle Rushen, which dates from the early twelfth century, emphasize the influence of the Scandinavians in the Irish Sea, but it is the intangibles – language, law, Church and constitution – that positively confirm the importance of the Norse heritage of he Isle of Man.

8 Cain 1996, 321-2.

SOURCES

Abramson, P. 2000. 'A re-examination of a Viking Age burial at Beacon Hill, Aspatria', *Transactions of the Cumberland and Westmorland Antiquarian and Archaeological Society*, n.s.100, 79-88.

Anderson, J. 1906-7. 'Notice of bronze brooches and personal ornaments from a ship-burial of Viking time in Oronsay … and Colonsay', *Proceedings of the Society of Antiquaries of Scotland*, 41, 437-50.

Arbman, H. 1940. *Birka I. Die Gräber*. Stockholm.

Bailey, R. 1980. *Viking Age sculpture in northern England*, London.

Bailey, R. 1986. 'Aspects of Viking-Age sculpture in Cumbria', in J. R. Baldwin and I. D. Whyte (eds.), *The Scandinavians in Cumbria*, Edinburgh, 53-64.

Bailey, R. 1996. *England's earliest sculptors*, Toronto. Publications of the Dictionary of Old English, 5.

Bailey, R. 1996a. 'What mean these stones? Some aspects of pre-Norman sculpture in Cheshire and Lancashire', *Bulletin of the John Rylands Library of Manchester*, 78, 21-46.

Bailey, R. N. and R. Cramp 1988. *Cumberland, Westmorland and Lancashire North-of-the-Sands*, Oxford. The British Academy corpus of Anglo-Saxon sculpture, 2.

Barnes, M. P. 1993. 'Norse in the British Isles', in A. Faulkes and R. Perkins (eds.), *Viking revaluations*, London, 65-84.

Barnes, M. P. 1994. The *runic inscriptions of Maeshowe, Orkney*, Uppsala. Runrön. Runologiska bidrag utgivna av Institutionen för nordiska språk vid Uppsala universitetet, 8.

Barnes, M. P. and R. I. Page 2006. The *Scandinavian runic inscriptions of Britain*, Uppsala. Runrön. Runologiska bidrag utgivna av Institutionen för nordiska språk vid Uppsala universitetet, 19.

Barnwell, E. L. 1868. 'Notes on the stone monuments in the Isle of Man', in Cumming 1868, 92-106.

Barton, R. 1999. 'Manx granite-tempered ware', in Davey 1999, 221-40.

Bersu, G. 1949. 'A promontory fort on the shore of Ramsey Bay, Isle of Man', *The Antiquaries journal*, 29, 62-79.

Bersu, G. 1970-2. 'Chapel Hill – a prehistoric, Early-Christian and Viking site at Balladoole, Kirk Arbory, Isle of Man', *Proceedings of the Isle of Man Natural History and Antiquarian Society*, n.s. 7:4, 632-65.

Bersu, G. and D. M. Wilson 1966. *Three Viking graves in the Isle of Man*, London 1966. The Society for Medieval Archaeology, Monograph Series, 1.

Bill, J. 2005. 'Kiloran Bay revisited – confirmation of a doubtful boat grave' in Mortensen and Arge (eds.), 345-58.

Blackburn, M. A. S. (ed.). 1986. *Anglo-Saxon monetary history. Essays in honour of Michael Dolley*, Leicester.

Blackburn, M. A. S. 2007. 'Gold in England during 'the age of silver'', in J. Graham-Campbell and G. Williams (eds.) 2007. *Silver economy in the Viking Age*, Walnut Creek, 55-98.

Blackburn, M. A. S. and H. Pagan 1986. 'A revised check-list of coin-hoards from the British Isles *c.* 500-1100' in Blackburn 1986, 291-314.

Blair, J. 2005. *The Church in Anglo-Saxon society*. Oxford.

Bøe, J. 1940. *Norse antiquities in Ireland*, Oslo. Viking antiquities in Great Britain and Ireland (ed. H. Shetelig), 3.

Bornholdt, K. A. 1999. 'Myth or mint. The evidence for a Viking-age coinage in the Isle of Man', in Davey 1999, 199-220.

Bornholdt, K. A. 2007. 'Coinage', in Duffy 2007, 466-83.

Bornholdt, see also Collins.

Bourke, C. 1993. 'The chronology of Irish crucifixion plaques', in R. M. Spearman and J. Higgitt (eds.) *The age of migrating ideas. Early medieval art in Northern Britain and Ireland*. Edinburgh 1993, 175-181.

Brink, S. 2003. 'Legal assemblies and judicial structure in early Scandinavia', in P. S. Barnwell and M. Mostert (eds.), *Political assemblies in the earlier Middle Ages*, Turnhout 2003, 61-72.

Brink, S. 2004. 'Legal assembly sites in early Scandinavia' in Pantos and Semple 2004, 205-16.

Britnell, W. J. 1990. 'Capel Maelog, Llandrindod Wells, Powys: excavations 1984-87', *Medieval Archaeology*, 34, 27-96.

Broderick, G. 1979. *Cronica regum Manniae et Insularum*, [Douglas].

Broderick, G. 2000. *Placenames of the Isle of Man*, 5, Tübingen.

Broderick, G. 2002. *Placenames of the Isle of Man*, 6, Tübingen.

Broderick, G. 2003. 'Tynwald: a Manx cult-site and institution of pre-Scandinavian origin', *Cambrian medieval Celtic studies*, 46, 55-94.

Brøgger, A. W. *et al.* 1917. *Osebergfunnet*, 1, Kristiania.

Brøgger, A. W. and H. Shetelig 1971. *The Viking ships; their ancestry and evolution*, 2 ed., Oslo.

Brøndsted, J. 1936. 'Danish inhumation graves of the Viking Age. A survey', *Acta archaeologica*, 7, 81-228.

Bruce, J. R. and W. Cubbon 1930. 'Cronk yn How: an early Christian and Viking site at Lezayre, Isle of Man', *Archaeologia Cambrensis*, 85, 267-308.

Byrne, F. J. 1973. *Irish Kings and High-Kings*. London.

Cain, W. 1996. 'Constitutional reform in the twentieth century', *Proceedings of the Isle of Man Natural History and Antiquarian Socitey*, 10:3, 201-24.

Carver, M. 2005. *Sutton Hoo. A seventh-century princely burial in its context*, London. Reports of the Research Committee of the Society of Antiquaries of London, 69.

Chadwick, R. A. *et al.* 2001. *Geology of the Isle of Man and its offshore area*, Keyworth. British Geological Survey research report RR/01/06.

Charles-Edwards, T. M. 2000. *Early Christian Ireland*, Cambridge.

Chiverrell, R. and G. Thomas 2006. *Evolution of the natural landscape*, Liverpool. A new history of the Isle of Man, 1.

Christensen, A. E. *et al.* 1992. *Osebergs-Dronningens grav. Vår arkeologiske nasjonalskatt i nytt lys*, Oslo.

Christensen, A. E. and M. Nockert 2006, *Osebergfunnet* 4, Oslo.

Christensen, T. 1981. 'Gerdrup-graven', *ROMU II. Årsskrift for Roskilde Museum*, 19-28.

Christensen, T. and Bennike, P. 1983. 'Kvinder for fred', *Skalk,* 1983:3, 9-11.

Clarke, H. B. *et al.* (eds.) 1998. *Ireland and Scandinavia in the early Viking Age*, Dublin.

Coles, F. R. 1892-3. 'The motes, forts and doons in the east and west divisions of the Stewartry of Kircudbright', *Proceedings of the Society of Antiquaries of Scotland,* 27, 92-182.

Collingwood, W. G. 1927. *Northumbrian crosses of the pre-Norman age*, London.

Collins, K.A. Bornholdt 2003. *Viking-Age coin finds from the Isle of Man. A study of coin circulation, production and concepts of wealth*, Unpublished PhD thesis, Cambridge.

Cowper, H. S. 1891. 'Law Ting at Fell Foot, Little Langdale, Westmorland', *Transactions of the Cumberland and Westmorland Antiquarian and Archaeological Society*, 11, 1-6.

Crawford, B. 1987. *Scandinavian Scotland*, Leicester.

Crawford, B. 2007. 'Man in the Norse world', in Duffy 2007, 210-40.

Cubbon, A. M. 1965. 'A Viking Sword from Ballabrooie, Patrick,' *Journal of the Manx Museum*, vi:81, 249-53.

Cubbon, A. M. 1978-80. 'Find of a Viking sword, spear and shield from Claghbane, Ramsey, Isle of Man', *Proceedings of the Isle of Man Natural History and Antiquarian Society*, 8:4, 439-51.

Cubbon, A. M. 1982. 'The early church in the Isle of Man', in S. M. Pearce (ed.), *The early church in western Britain and Ireland*, Oxford, 257-82. BAR British Series 102.

Cubbon, A. M. 1983. 'The archaeology of the Vikings in the Isle of Man', in Fell *et al.*, 1983. 13-26.

Cubbon, A. M. 1997-9. 'A remarkable decade of Manx coin hoards', *Proceedings of the Isle of Man Natural History and Antiquarian Society*, 11:1, 29-50.

Cubbon, A. M. 1999-2000. 'A Viking-age plaited gold finger-ring from Greeba, Isle of Man', *Proceedings of the Isle of Man Natural History and Antiquarian Society*, 11:2, 249-57.

Cumming, J. G. (ed.) 1868. *Antiquitates Manniæ*, i. Douglas. Manx Society, 15.

Curle, A. O. *et al.* 1954. *Civilisation of the Viking Settlers in relation to their old and new countries*, Oslo. Viking Antiquities in Great Britain and Ireland (ed. H. Shetelig), 6.

Darvill, T. 2001. *Billown Neolithic landscape project, Isle of Man. Sixth Report: 2000,* Bournemouth and Douglas. Bournemouth University School of Conservation Sciences. Research Report 9.

Darvill, T. 2004. 'Tynwald Hill and the 'things' of power', in Pantos and Semple 2004, 217-32.

Davey, P. J. (ed.) 1978. *Man and environment in the Isle of Man*, Oxford. British Archaeological Reports, British Series 54.

Davey, P. J. *et al.* 1995. *Kerrowdhoo, Bride, Isle of Man: field work and excavation 1992-1994*. Douglas. Centre for Manx Studies, research report 4.

Davey, P. J. 1999. *Recent archaeological research in the Isle of Man*, Oxford. British Archaeological Reports, British Series 278.

Davey, P. J. and D. Finlayson 2002. *Mannin revisited, Twelve essays on Manx culture and environment*. Edinburgh.

Davies, W. 1990. *Patterns of power in early Wales*, Oxford.

Davies, W. 1992. 'The myth of the Celtic Church', in Edwards and Lane 1992, 12-21.

Ditchburn, D. and B. T. Hudson 2007. 'Economy and trade in medieval Man', in Duffy 2007, 377-410.

Dolley, R. H. M. 1975. 'Some preliminary observations on three Manx coin-hoards appearing to end with pennies of Eadgar' *Spink's numismatic circular*, 190-2.

Dolley, R. H. M. 1976. 'The coins', in Wilson 1976, 349-72.

Doonan, R. C. P. *et al.* 2001. 'Investigations at Langness: the 2000 field-season', in Darvill 2001, 40-7.

Draskau, J. K. 2006. *Account of the Isle of Man in song*. Douglas. Centre for Manx Studies Monograph 5.

Driscoll, S. 1997. 'Kingdom of Strathclyde's final chapter', *British Archaeology*, 27,6.

Duffy, S. (ed.) 2007 [forthcoming], *A new history of the Isle of Man*, iii, *the medieval period 1000-1406*, Liverpool.

Dumville, D. N. (ed.) 1985. *The Historia Brittonum. 3, the 'Vatican' recension*. Cambridge.

Edwards, B. J. N. 1992. 'The Vikings in north-west England: The archaeological evidence', in Graham-Campbell 1992, 43-62.

Edwards, N. 1990. *The archaeology of early medieval Ireland*, London.

Edwards, N. 1999. 'Viking-influenced sculpture in North Wales, its ornamental context', *Church archaeology* 3, 5-16.

Edwards, N. 2005. 'The archaeology of early medieval Ireland, *c.* 400-1169', in Ó Cróinín 2005, 235-300.

Edwards N. and A. Lane (eds.) 1992. *The early Church in Wales and the West*, Oxford. Oxbow monograph 16.

Eldjárn, K. 1956. *Kuml og Haugfé*, Reykjavík.

Ewing, T. 2006. *Viking clothing*, Stroud.

Fanning, T. 1983. 'The Hiberno-Norse pins from the Isle of Man', in Fell *et al.* 1983, 27-36.

Fanning, T. 1994. *Viking Age ringed pins from Dublin*, Dublin 1994. Medieval Dublin Excavations 1962-81, ser. B,4.

Fell, C. E. 1986. 'Old English *Wicing*. A question of semantics', *Proceedings of the British Academy*, 71, 295-316.

Fell, C. E. 1987. 'Modern English *Viking*', *Leeds Studies in English*, 111-23.

Fell, C. E. *et al.* (eds.) 1983. *The Viking Age in the Isle of Man*, London. Select papers from the ninth Viking Congress.

Fellows-Jensen, G. 1983. 'Scandinavian settlement in the Isle of Man and Northwest England: the place-name evidence', in Fell *et al.* 1983, 37-52.

Fellows-Jensen, G. 1993. 'Tingwall, Dingwall, and Thingwall', *Nowele*, 21-2, 53-67. (Also published as *Twenty-eight papers presented to Hans Bekker-Nielsen on the occasion of his sixtieth birthday, 28 April 1993*, Odense.)

Fellows-Jensen, G. 1996. '*Tingwall*: the significance of the name', in D. J. Waugh, *Shetland's northern links. Language and history*, Edinburgh, 16-27.

Fellows-Jensen, G. 2001. 'The mystery of the *bý*-names in Man', *Nomina*, 24, 33-46.

Fellows-Jensen, G. 2001-3. 'How old are the Scandinavian place-names in Man?' *Proceedings of the Isle of Man Natural History and Antiquarian Society*, 11,3, 423-36.

Fellows-Jensen, G. 2002. 'Toponymie maritime scandinave en Angleterre, au Pays de Galles et sur L'île de Man, in E. Ridel (ed.) *L'héritage maritime des Vikings en Europe de l'Ouest*, Caen, 401-22.

Fellows-Jensen, G. 2007. 'The Manx place-name evidence', in Duffy 2007, 254-80.

Feltham, J. 1798. *A tour through the Isle of Mann in 1797 and 1798*, Bath.

Fisher, I. 2001. *Early medieval sculpture in the West Highlands and Islands*, Edinburgh. Royal Commission on the Ancient and Historical Monuments in Scotland and The Society of Antiquaries of Scotland, monograph series, 1.

Fleure, H. J. and M. Dunlop 1942. 'Glendarragh Circle and Alignments, the Braaid, I.O.M', *The Antiquaries journal*, 22, 39-53.

Foote, P. G. and D. M.Wilson 1970. *The Viking achievement*, London.

Fox, A. and K. Bornholdt Collins 2004. 'A Manx silver hoard from Glenfaba, Isle of Man', *Viking heritage magazine*, 1:04, 3-5.

Freke, D. 2002. *Excavations on St Patrick's Isle, Peel, Isle of Man, 1982-88, Prehistoric, Medieval and later*, Liverpool. Centre for Manx Studies Monographs 2.

Fuglesang, S. H. 1991. 'The axehead from Mammen and the Mammen style', in Iversen 1991, 163-80.

Fuglesang, S. H. 2005. 'Runesteinenes ikonografi', *Hikuin* 32, 75-94.

Gelling, P. S. 1952. 'Excavation of a promontory fort at Port Grenaugh, Santon', *Proceedings of the Isle of Man Natural History and Antiquarian Society*, 5:3, 307-15.

Gelling, P. S. 1957. 'Excavation of a promontory fort at Scarlett, Castletown, Isle of Man', *Proceedings of the Isle of Man Natural History and Antiquarian Society*, 5:5, 571-5.

Gelling, P. S. 1959. 'Excavation of a promontory fort at Cass ny Hawin, Malew, Isle of Man', *Proceedings of the Isle of Man Natural History and Antiquarian Society*, 6:1, 28-38.

Gelling, P. S. 1962-3. 'Medieval shielings in the Isle of Man', *Medieval archaeology*, 6-7, 136-72.

Gelling, P. S. 1964. 'The Braaid Site' *Journal of the Manx Museum*, 6, 201-5.

Gelling, P. S. 1970. 'A Norse homestead near Doarlish Cashen, Kirk Patrick, Isle of Man', *Medieval archaeology*, 14, 74-82.

Goodall, J. 2004. 'Manx arms and seals revisited', *Proceedings of the Isle of Man Natural History and Antiquarian Society*, xi;3, 441-52.

Graham-Campbell, J. 1983. 'Viking-Age silver hoards of the Isle of Man', in Fell *et al.* 1983, 53-80.

Graham-Campbell, J. (ed.) 1992. *Viking Treasure from the north-west. The Cuerdale Hoard in its context*, Liverpool. National Museums and Galleries on Merseyside, Occasional Papers: Liverpool Museum No. 5.

Graham-Campbell, J. 1995. *The Viking-Age gold and silver of Scotland (AD 850-1100)*, Edinburgh.

Graham-Campbell, J. 1998. 'The Early Viking Age in the Irish Sea area', in Clarke 1998, 104-30.

Graham-Campbell, J. 2001. *Whithorn and the Viking world*, Whithorn. 8th. Whithorn lecture.

Graham-Campbell, J. 2005. 'The Viking-Age gold and silver in the North Atlantic Region', in Mortensen and Arge 2005, 125-40.

Graham-Campbell, J. forthcoming. *The Cuerdale hoard and related Viking-Age silver and gold, from Britain and Ireland, in the British Museum*, London.

Graham-Campbell, J. and C. E. Batey 1998. *Vikings in Scotland, an archaeological survey*, Edinburgh.

Graham-Campbell, J. and J. Sheehan (2003-5). 'A Viking-Age silver hoard of "ring-money" from the Isle of Man rediscovered', *Proceedings of the Isle of Man Natural History and Antiquarian Society.* 11:4, 527-40.

Grandell, A. 'Finds from Bryggen indicating business transactions', *The Bryggen papers, supplementary ser.* 2, 66-72.

Grieg, S. 1940. *Viking antiquities in Scotland.* Oslo. Viking antiquities in Great Britain and Ireland (ed. H. Shetelig), 2.

Griffiths, D. 1992. 'The coastal trading ports of the Irish Sea', in Graham-Campbell 1992, 63-72.

Griffiths, D. 2001. 'Great sites. Meols', *British archaeology*, 62, 20-25.

Griffiths, D., G. Egan and R. Philpotts 2007. *Meols: the archaeology of the north-west Wirral Coast*, Oxford. University School of Archaeology Monograph Series, 68.

Hadley, D. M. 2002. 'Burial practices in northern England in the later Anglo-Saxon period', in Lucy and Reynolds (eds.), 2002, 209-28.

Hadley, D. M and J. D. Richards (eds.) 2000. *Cultures in contact: Scandinavian settlement in England in the ninth and tenth centuries*, Turnhout 2000.

Halsall, G. 1992. 'The Viking presence in England? The burial evidence', in Hadley and Richards 2000, 259-76.

Hamilton, J. R. C. 1956. *Excavations at Jarlshof, Shetland*, Edinburgh.

Harbison, P. 1984. 'The bronze crucifixion plaque, said to be from St. John's (Rinnagan), near Athlone', *Journal of Irish archaeology*, 2, 1-17.

Harrison, S. H. 2000. 'The Millhill burial in context', *Acta Archaeologica* 71, 65-78. Acta Archaeologica Supplementa, 2.

Harrison, S. H. 2001. 'Viking graves and grave-goods in Ireland', in Larsen 2001, 61-75.

Harrison, S. H. 2005. 'College Green – a neglected 'Viking' cemetery at Dublin', in Mortensen and Arge 2005, 329-39.

Harrison, W. 1871. *Records of the Tynwald & Saint John's chapels in the Isle of Man*, Douglas. The Manx Society 19.

HE. *Bede's Ecclesiastical history of the English people*, (B. Colgrave and R. A. B. Mynors eds.). Oxford 1969.

Henry, F. 1967. *Irish art during the Viking invasions (800-1020 A.D.)*, London.

Higgins, D.A. 1999, 'Survey and trial excavations at the 'Ronalsdsway Village' site, Ronaldsway Airport, Isle of Man', in Davey 1999, 139-52.

Higham, M. C. 1978. 'The 'Erg' place-names of northern England', in Davey 1978, 347-56.

Hill, P. 1997. *Whithorn and St. Ninians. The excavation of a monastic town 1984-91*, Stroud.

Hohler, E. B. 1999. *Norwegian stave church sculpture*, Oslo.

Holgate, B. 1987. *Pagan lady of Peel*, n.p.

Hughes, K. 2005. 'The Church in Irish society, 400-800', in Ó Cróinín 2005, 301-30.

Iversen, M. (ed.) 1991. *Mammen. Grav, kunst og samfund i vikingetid*, Højbjerg. Jysk Arkæologisk Selskabs Skrifter, 28.

Jacobsen, L. 1933. *Evje-stenen og Alstad-stenen*, Oslo. Norske Oldfunn, 6.

Jansson, S. B. F. 1987. *Runes in Sweden*, 2 ed. Stockholm.

Jesch, J. 1991. *Women in the Viking Age*, Woodbridge.

Johnson, A. 1997-9. 'A view from the hills – Some thoughts on the reoccupation of promontory forts and the possible origins of the Manx farmstead', *Proceedings of the Isle of Man Natural History and Antiquarian Society*, 11:1, 51-66.

Johnson, A. 1999. 'A preliminary gazetteer of early archaeological remains in the Upper Sulby Valley' in Davey 1999, 153-70.

Johnson, A. 2002. 'Watch and Ward on the Isle of Man. The medieval re-occupation of Iron Age promontory forts', in Davey and Finlayson 2002, 63-80.

Jondell, E. 1974. *Vikingatidens balansvågar i Norge*, Uppsala. C 1-uppsats i arkeologi, särskilt nordeuropeisk.

Jones, H. 1992. 'Early medieval cemeteries in Wales', in Edwards and Lane 1992, 92-104.

Jonsson, K. 1987. *The new era. The reformation of the late Anglo-Saxon coinage*. Stockholm/London. Commentationes de nummis saeculorum IX-XI in suecia repertis, n.s.1.

Kavanagh, R. M. 1988. 'The horse in Viking Ireland', in J. Bradley (ed.) *Settlement and society in medieval Ireland. Studies presented to F. X. Martin o.s.a.* Kilkenny, 89-122.

Kelly, T. A. D. 1994. 'The Govan collection in the context of local history', in A. Ritchie (ed.) *Govan and its early medieval sculpture*, Stroud, 1-17.

Kermode, P. M. C. 1930. 'Ship-burial in the Isle of Man', *The Antiquaries journal*, 10, 126-33.

Kermode, P. M. C. 1994. *Manx crosses*, 2 ed. Balgavies.

Kieffer-Olson, J. 2004. 'Tidlige kirkegårde, struktur og gravskik', in Lund 2004, 174-80.

KLNM. Kulturhistorisk Leksikon for nordisk middelalder, København, 1956-78.

Kruse, S. E. 1988. 'Ingots and weight units in Viking Age silver hoards', *World Archaeology*, 20, 285-301.

Lang, J. T. 1984. 'The hogback. A Viking colonial monument', *Anglo-Saxon studies in archaeology and history*, 3, 86-176.

Larsen, A.-C. (ed.) 2001. *The Vikings in Ireland*, Roskilde.

Larsson, G. 2007. *Ship and society. Maritime ideology in Late Iron Age Sweden*, Uppsala. Aun 37.

Liestøl, A. 1983. 'An Iona rune-stone and the world of Man and the Isles', in Fell *et al.* 1983, 85-94.

Lindqvist, S. 1941. *Gotlands Bildsteine*, Stockholm.

Lowe, C. 1987. *Early ecclesiastical sites in the Northern Isles and the Isle of Man: an archaeological field survey*, Cambridge. (Unpublished PhD thesis.)

Lucy, S. and A. Reynolds (eds.) 2002. *Burial in early medieval England and Wales*, London. Society for Medieval Archaeology Monograph, 17.

Lund, N. (ed.) 2004. *Kristendommen i Danmark før 1050*, Roskilde.

Lunt, D. A. 1989-91. 'The age of the Viking from Ballateare, Jurby, report on dentition', *Proceedings of the Isle of Man Natural History and Antiquarian Society*, 10:1, 162-3.

Lyngstrøm, H. 1993. 'Ketting – en vikingetids gravplads med ryttergrave', *Aarbøger for nordisk oldkyndighed og historie*, 1993, 143-80.

Margeson, S. 1983. 'On the iconography of the Manx crosses', in Fell *et al.* 1983, 95-106.

Marstrander, C. J. S. 1932. 'Det norske landnåm på Man', *Norsk tidskrift for sprogvitenskap*, 6, 40-386.

Marstrander, C. J. S. 1937. 'Treen og keeil: et førnorsk jorddelingsprinsip på Britiske Øyene', *Norsk tidskrift før sprogvitenskap*, 8, 287-500.

Megaw, B. R. S. 1935-7. 'Weapons of the Viking Age found in Man', *Journal of the Manx Museum*, 3, 234-6.

M[egaw], B. R. S. 1937. 'A list of ancient beads found in the Isle of Man', *Journal of the Manx Museum*, 3, 237.

M[egaw], B. R. S. 1938. 'An ancient cemetery at Balladoyne St John's. New discoveries near Tynwald Hill', *Journal of the Manx Museum*, 4, 11-14.

Megaw, B. R. S. 1943, 'The Manx pony: a descendant of the British prehistoric horse', *Journal of the Manx Museum*, 5:68, 100-3.

Megaw, B. R. S. 1959-60. 'The ship seals of the Kings of Man', *Journal of the Manx Museum*, 6:6, 78-80.

Megaw, B. R. S. 1976. 'Norsemen and native in the kingdom of the Isles. A re-assessment of the Manx evidence', *Scottish Studies*, 20, 1-44.

Megaw, B. R. S. 1978. 'Norsemen and native in the kingdom of the Isles. A re-assessment of the Manx evidence' in Davey, 1978, 265-314. [A slightly revised version of Megaw 1976.]

Megaw, B. R. S. and E. M. Megaw (1950). 'The Norse heritage in the Isle of Man', in C. Fox and B. Dickins (eds.), *The early centuries of north-west Europe (H. M. Chadwick memorial studies)*, Cambridge, 141-70.

Megaw, E. M. 1978. 'The Manx 'eary' and its significance', in Davey 1978, 327-45.

Metcalf, D. M. 1980. 'Continuity and social change in English monetary history *c.* 973-1086, part 1', *British Numismatic Journal* 50, 20-49.

Metcalf, D. M. 1981, 'Continuity and social change in English monetary history *c.* 973-1086. Part 2' *British Numismatic Journal* 51, 52-90.

Metcalf, D. M. 1986. 'The monetary history of England in the tenth century viewed in the perspective of the eleventh century', in Blackburn 1986,133-58.

Metcalf, D. M. 1992. 'The monetary economy of the Irish Sea province', in Graham-Campbell 1992, 89-106.

Moore, R. H. 1999. 'The Manx multiple estate: evidence for undertones', in Davey 1999, 171-82.

Morris, C. D. 1983. 'The survey and excavations at Keeill Vael, Druidale, in their context', in Fell *et al.* 1983, 107-32.

Morris, C. D. 1989. *Church and monastery in the far north: the archaeological evidence*, Jarrow. Jarrow Lecture.

Mortensen, A. and Arge, S. V. (eds.) 2005. *Viking and Norse in the North Atlantic. Select papers from the fourteenth Viking Congress…* Tórshavn.

Müller-Wille, M. 1974. Boat-graves in northern Europe', *The International Journal of Nautical and Underwater Exploration*, 3:2, 187-204.

Müller-Wille, M. 1976. 'Das Bootkammergrab von Haithabu', *Berichte über die Ausgrabungen in Haithabu*, 8.

Müller-Wille, M. 1995. 'Boat-graves, old and new views', in O. Crumlin-Pedersen and B. M. Thye (eds.) *The ship as symbol in prehistoric and medieval Scandinavia*, Copenhagen. Publications from the National Museum. Studies in Archaeology and History, 1.

Müller-Wille, M. 2002. 'Das Bootgrab
von Balladoole, Isle of Man', *Deutsches
Schiffahrtsarkiv,* 25, 295-310.

Nash-Williams, V. E. 1950. *The Early
Christian Monuments of Wales,* Cardiff.

Neely, G. J. H. 1940. 'Excavations at
Ronaldsway, Isle of Man', *The Antiquaries
journal,* 20, 72-86.

Nelson, J. L. 2003. 'England and the
Continent in the ninth century; II, the
Vikings and Others', *Transactions of the
Royal Historical Society,* 6 ser. 13, 1-28.

Nicolaysen, N. 1882. *The Viking-ship
discovered at Gokstad in Norway,*
Christiania.

Norman, E. R. and J. K. St Joseph 1969.
*The early development of Irish society,
the evidence of aerial photography,*
Cambridge. Cambridge Air Surveys 3.

O'Brien, E. 1992. 'A re-assessment of the
'great sepulchral mound' containing a
Viking burial at Donnybrook, Dublin',
Medieval archaeology, 36, 170-74.

O'Brien, E. 1998. 'The location and context
of Viking burials at Kilmainham and
Islandbridge, Dublin' in Clarke *et al.*
1998, 203-21.

Ó Corráin, D. 1997. 'Ireland, Wales, Man and
the Hebrides', in Sawyer 1997, 83-109.

Ó Corráin, D. 1998.'The Vikings in Scotland
and Ireland in the ninth century', *Peritia,*
xii, 296-339.

Ó Cróinín, D. (ed.). 2005. *A new history of
Ireland,* 1. *Prehistoric and early Ireland,*
Oxford 2005.

Ó Floinn, R. 1998. 'The archaeology of the
early Viking Age in Ireland', in Clarke *et
al.* 1998, 131-65

Olsen, M. 1954. 'Runic inscriptions in Great
Britain, Ireland and the Isle of Man', in
Curle *et al.* 1954, 151-234.

Olsen, O. 1966. *Hørg, hov og kirke.*
København. (*Aarbøger for nordisk
Oldkyndighed og Historie,* 1965).

Olsen, O. and H. Schmidt 1977. *Fyrkat. En
jysk vikingeborg.* I. *Borgen og bebyggelsen,*
København. Nordiske Fortidsminder,
serie B – in quarto, 3.

Ó Riordáin, B. 1976. 'The High Street
excavations', in B. Almqvist and D.
Greene (eds.), *Proceedings of the Seventh
Viking Congress,* Dublin, 135-40.

Oswald, H. R. 1860. *Vestigia insulæ manniæ
antiquiora ...,* Douglas. The Manx
Society, v.

Owen, O. 2004. 'The Scar boat burial – and
the missing decades of the early Viking
Age in Shetland and Orkney', in J.
Adams and K. Holman, *Scandinavia and
Europe 800-1350. Contact, conflict and
Coexistence,* Turnhout 2004, 3-34.

Owen, O. and M. Dalland 1999. *Scar, a
Viking boat burial on Sanday, Orkney,*
East Linton.

Pagan, H. E. 1981. 'The 1894 Ballaquayle
hoard: five further parcels of coins
Æthelstan-Eadgar', *British Numismatic
Journal,* 50, 12-19.

Page, R. I. 1983. 'The Manx rune-stones', in
Fell *et al.* 1983, 133-46. (Reprinted in Page
1995, 225-44).

Page, R. I. 1995. *Runes and runic inscriptions,*
Woodbridge.

Page, R. I. 1999. *An introduction to English
runes,* 2 ed., Woodbridge.

Pantos, A. and S. Semple (eds.) 2004.
*Assembly places and practices in medieval
Europe,* Dublin.

Paterson, C. 2001. 'Insular belt-fittings
from pagan Norse graves in Scotland: a
reappraisal in the light of scientific and
stylistic analysis,' in M. Redknap *et al.,*
(eds.). *Pattern and purpose in insular art,*
Oxford, 125-32.

Pedersen, A. 1997. 'Weapons and riding gear in burials – evidence of social rank in 10th century Denmark?', in A. N. Jørgensen and B. L. Clausen (eds.), *Military aspects of Scandinavian society in a European perspective, AD 1-1300*, Copenhagen. Publications from the National Museum. Studies in archaeology & history, 2.

Pedersen, A. 2002. 'Prachtgräber des 10 Jahrhunderts in Südskandinavien – Tradition und Erneuerung', in J. Henning (ed.), *Europa im 10. Jahrhundert. Archäologie einer Aufbruchszeit*, Mainz, 81-94.

Pedersen, A, 2006. 'Ancient mounds for new graves. An aspect of Viking Age burial custom in southern Scandinavia', in A. Andrén, *et al.*, (eds.), *Old Norse religion in long-term perspectives. Origins, changes, and interactions,* Lund 2006, 346-53.

Peirce, I. C. 2002. *Swords of the Viking Age.* Woodbridge.

Pelteret, D. 1981. 'Slave raiding and slave-trading in early England', *Anglo-Saxon England*, 9, 99-114,

Petersen, J. 1919. *De norske vikingesverd. En typlogoisk-kronologisk studie over Vikingetidens Vaaben*, Kristiania. Videnskapsselskaps Skrifter. II. Hist.-Filos. Klasse. No 1.

Petersen, J. 1951. *Vikingetidens Redskaper,* Oslo. Skrifter utgitt av det Norske Videnskaps-Akedemi i Oslo. II. Hist.-Filos Klasse. No 2.

Potter, T. W. and R. D. Andrews 1994. 'Excavation and survey at St. Patrick's Chapel and St. Peter's Church, Heysham, Lancashire, 1977-8', *The Antiquaries journal*, 74, 53-134.

Power, R. 2005. 'Norse-Gaelic relations in the Kingdom of Man and the Isles, 1090-1270', *Saga Book*, 5-66.

Price, N. S. 2002. *The Viking way. Religion and war in late Iron Age Scandinavia*, Uppsala. Aun 31.

Quartermaine, J. and M. Krupa 1994. *Thingmount, Cumbria*, Lancaster. Report, Lancaster University Archaeological Unit for the National Trust.

Quayle, B. 1794. *General view of agriculture in the Isle of Man,* London. (Reprinted, Douglas 1992).

Raftery, B. 2005. 'Iron-age Ireland', in Ó Cróinín 2005, 134-81.

Rahtz, P. 1976. 'Buildings and rural settlement', in Wilson 1976, 49-98.

Ramskou, T. 1965. 'Vikingerne ofrede mennesker', *Nationalmuseets Arbejdsmark*, 79-86.

Redknap, M. 2000. *Vikings in Wales, an archaeological quest,* Cardiff.

Reilly, P. 1988. *Computer analysis of an archaeological landscape. Medieval land divisions in the Isle of Man.* Oxford. BAR British Series 190.

Richards, J. D. 2002. 'The case of the missing Vikings. Scandinavian burial in the Danelaw', in Lucy and Richards, 156-70.

Richards, J. D. 2004. 'Excavations at the Viking barrow cemetery at Heath Wood, Ingleby, Derbyshire', *The Antiquaries journal*, 84, 23 -116

Roesdahl, E. 1980. *Danmarks vikingetid,* [København].

Roesdahl, E. 1993. 'Pagan beliefs, Christian impact and archaeology – a Danish view', in A. Faulkes and R. Perkins (eds.) *Viking revaluations. Viking Society centenary symposium 14-15 May 1992,* London, 128-36.

Roesdahl, E. 1997. 'Landscape sculpture in the Viking Age', *Aarhus Geoscience*, 7, 147-55.

Roesdahl, E. 2005. 'Jordfaste mindesmærker i Danmarks yngre vikingetid', *Hikuin* 32, 55-74.

Roesdahl, E. 2006. 'Aristocratic burial in late Viking Age Denmark. Custom, regionality, conversion,' in C. von Carnap-Bornheim *et al.* (ed.) *Herrschaft – Tod – Bestattung*, Bonn. Universitätsforschungen zur prähistorischen Archäologie, 139, 169-83.

Rowe, H. M. 1967. 'A carved stone at Castledermot, Co. Kildare', *Journal of the Royal Society of Antiquaries of Ireland* 97, 179-80.

Rygh, O. 1885, *Norske Oldsager*, Christiania.

Sawyer, P. (ed.) 1997. *The Oxford illustrated history of the Vikings*, Oxford.

Schmale, F. J. and I. Schmale-Ott (eds.) 1972. *Frutulfs und Ekkehards Chroniken*, Darmstadt.

Schmidt, H. 1994. *Building customs in Viking Age Denmark*, [Herning].

Scott, T. and P. Starkey (eds.) 1995. *The Middle Ages in the North West*, Oxford and Liverpool.

Simpson, L. 2004. 'Viking Dublin: the ninth-century evidence begins to unfold – Temple Bar, Ship Street and South Great George's Street', *Beretning fra treogtyvende tværfaglige vikingesymposium*, 47-63.

Skaarup, J. 1976. *Stengade II. En langelandsk gravplads...*, Rudkøbing.

Skinner, F. J. and R. L. S. Bruce-Mitford 1940. 'A Celtic balance-beam of the Christian period', *The Antiquaries Journal*, 20, 87-102.

Skre, D. (ed.) 2007. *Kaupang in Skiringssal*, Oslo/Aarhus. Kaupang excavation project, 1. Norske Oldfunn 22.

Sørensen, P. Meulengracht 1997. 'Religions old and new', in Sawyer 1997, 202-24.

Stalley, R. 2005. 'Ecclesiastical architecture in Ireland before 1066', in Ó Cróinín 2005, 714-43.

Statutes of the Isle of Man (ed. J. F. Gill), London 1883.

Svanberg, F. 2003. *Death rituals in south-east Scandinavia AD 800-100*, Lund. Acta Archaeologica Lundensia ser. in 4°, 24.

Tarlow, S. 1997. 'The dread of something after death, violation and desecration in the Isle of Man in the tenth century', in J. Carman, ed. *Material Harm. Archaeological studies of war and violence*, Glasgow, 133-42.

Thomson, R. L. 1983. 'The continuity of Manx', in Fell *et al.* 1983, 169-74.

Thomson R. L. 2007. 'Language in Man: prehistory to literacy', in Duffy 2007, 241-53.

Trench-Jellicoe, R. M. C. 1985. *Art-definition and stylistic analysis of P.M.C. Kermode's 'Pre-Scandinavian' series of Manx sculptured monuments*, Lancaster. (Unpublished PhD thesis.)

Trench-Jellicoe, R. M. C. 2002. 'Early Christian and Viking-Age sculptured monuments', in Freke 2002, 282-90.

Wamers, E. 1985. *Insularer Metallschmuck in wikingerzeitlichen Gräbern Nordeurapas. Untersuchungen zur scandinavischen Westexpansion*, Neumünster.

Warner, P. 1976. 'Scottish silver arm-rings: an analysis of weights', *Proceedings of the Society of Antiquaries of Scotland*, 107, 136-43.

Williams, B. 2007. 'The Chronicles of the Kingdom of Man and the Isles', in Duffy 2007, 305-28.

Williams, G. 2007. 'The system of land division and assessment', in Duffy 2007, 486-546.

Williams, H. 1997. 'Ancient landscapes and the dead: the reuse of prehistoric and Roman monuments as early Anglo-Saxon burial sites', *Medieval Archaeology*, 41, 1-32.

Wilson, D. M. 1967. 'The Vikings' relationship with Christianity in northern England', *Journal of the British Archaeological Association*, 3 ser., 30, 37-46

Wilson, D. M. 1974. *The Viking Age in the Isle of Man*, Odense. C.C. Rafn Lecture, 3.

Wilson, D. M. 1974a. 'Men de ligger i London', *Skalk*, nr. 5, 3-8.

Wilson, D. M. (ed.) 1976. *The archaeology of Anglo-Saxon England*, London.

Wilson, D. M. 1983. 'The art of the Manx crosses of the Viking Age', in Fell *et al.* 1983, 175-87.

Wilson, D. M. 1984. *Anglo Saxon art from the seventh century to the Norman Conquest*, London.

Wilson, D. M. 1995. *Vikingatidens konst*, Lund. Signums svenska konsthistoria: ii.

Wilson, D. M. 1995a. 'Scandinavian ornamental influence in the Irish Sea region in the Viking Age', in Scott and Starkey (eds.) 1995, 37-58.

Wilson, D. M. 1995/7. 'The chronology of the Viking Age in the Isle of Man', *Proceedings of the Isle of Man Natural History and Antiquarian Society*, 10: 4, 359-72.

Wilson, D. M. 2001/3. 'A ring from Greeba', *Proceedings of the Isle of Man Natural History and Antiquarian Society*, 11:3, 437-9.

Wilson, D. M. 2008. 'Stylistic influences in early Manx sculpture', in J. Graham-Campbell and M. Ryan (eds.) *Anglo-Saxon/Irish Relations before the Vikings*, London (forthcoming).

Wilson, D. M. 2008a. 'Early finds of Viking graves in the Isle of Man', in *Early medieval art and archaeology in the northern world* (forthcoming).

Wilson, D. M. and O. Klindt-Jensen 1966. *Viking Art*, London.

Woolf, A. 2007. 'The early history of the diocese of Sodor' in Duffy 2007, 329-48.

Wright, M. D. 1980-2. 'Excavation at Peel Castle, 1947', *Proceedings of the Isle of Man Natural History and Antiquarian Society*, 9:1, 21-58.

Zachrisson, I. 1993. 'Mötet mellan skandinaver och samer', *Beretning fra tolvte tværfaglige Vikingesymposium, Aarhus Universitet*, 7-22.

INDEX